CONSTITUTIONAL MUSINGS:

AN ANTHOLOGY OF LEGAL COLUMNS

NATHAN W. TUCKER

InArena Publishing House

Printed in the United States of America

This is an anthology of legal columns originally appearing in *The Iowa Republican*.

ISBN:9780615818009

InArena Publishing House

PREVIOUS PRAISE FOR NATHAN TUCKER

"I have to say, I'm always impressed with what you write." —Craig Robinson, editor of theiowarepublican.com

"Thank you...for your spirited argument, which advances the important argument." —George F. Will

"Brilliant...excellent." Jan Mickelson, host of WHO Radio's *Mickelson in the Morning*

"I think it is very, very good." —Steve Deace, syndicated talk radio host

"Your writing is smart and interesting." —*The Philadelphia Inquirer*

"Your command of the material is impressive." —*Akron Beacon Journal*

"I'm very impressed with your depth of thought, knowledge of history, and writing." —William C. Brown, partner at BrownWinick

DEDICATED TO ROBERT BORK'S AMERICA

CONTENTS

1 THE TASK OF JUDGING

AFFIRMATIVE ACTION FOR THE JUDICIARY?

(May 17, 2009)

In the days and weeks after U.S. Supreme Court Justice David Souter announced his retirement from the high court at the end of its current session, Beltway insiders have enthusiastically engaged in their favorite parlor game of speculating on who the next justice might be. Much has been made, rightfully so, of President Obama's comments that he wants to nominate empathetic judges to the federal bench. But little attention has been paid to the underlying assumption by pundits and commentators that Souter's replacement should be a woman, and preferably a Hispanic woman at that.

This belief that the Supreme Court, and, indeed, the entire federal judiciary, should be a model of affirmative action is not new. President George W. Bush was under intense pressure to nominate a female to replace the retiring Justice Sandra Day O'Connor, the first woman to sit on the Supreme Court. Bush, bowing to this pressure, nominated Harriet Miers to replace Justice O'Connor, a nomination which went from bad to worse and which was later withdrawn.

But as a new high court nomination cycle begins anew, many believe that after three straight confirmations of men (all of which, they would point out, are white), it is time for Justice Ruth Bader Ginsburg, the current court's lone female justice, to have another woman join her on the Court. As one commentator recently wrote in an op-ed in The Washington Post, "it's so essential that President Obama's nominee to replace David Souter be a woman." As this commentator freely admits, she is arguing that "no men need apply" for a seat on the Supreme Court. Why? Because, she argues, "the inescapable fact [is] that a female justice—like a justice who's a member of a racial minority...—brings a useful set of life experiences to the art of judging."

Under the rubric of "life experiences," however, is the insidious and prejudiced belief that all men and all women, as well as all members of a particular race, think alike and would rule on cases in the same way. Rather than looking solely at the merit of a particular nominee, proponents of affirmative action for the federal bench would categorize nominees by their gender and race and presume to know how they would vote on particular cases. Women are presumed to vote to uphold Roe v.

Wade, blacks are assumed to support the liberal civil rights agenda, and white men are for big business.

An example of this type of bigotry at work can be seen in the first President Bush's choice of Clarence Thomas to replace the first black Supreme Court Justice, Thurgood Marshall. The choice of a conservative black man to replace one of the most famous and influential civil rights lawyers of all time did not sit well among proponents of affirmative action for the judiciary.

This outrage on the left was not due to the fact that Thomas was simply a conservative, but that he was a black conservative who didn't get the memo that he was supposed to think a certain way and represent a certain constituency on the high court. He has been called "Uncle Tom Justice," diagnosed as a man who hated that fact that he was black, and the Reverend Al Sharpton once led a march to his house to "pray for Thomas' Black soul." But as Cynthia Tucker (no relation) of the Atlantic Journal and Constitution once put it, "Thomas is no less 'black' because he is ultraconservative. The notion that all blacks should think alike is ridiculous, stereotypical, and demeaning..."

However, not only does affirmative action for the judiciary categorize nominees by gender and race in violation of equal protection, but it transforms the law itself from blind, neutral justice to a consensus of life experiences. As Justice Antonin Scalia noted in an interview on CNBC shortly after O'Connor's retirement, "as far as the product of the court is concerned, [a female replacement] makes no difference at all. I don't think there's...a female legal answer to a question and a male legal answer to the same question. That's just silly."

The law should mean the same thing, regardless of the gender or race of the particular judge before which the case is heard. If it does not and the law can be manipulated by simply court-packing the federal bench with gender or racial clones who all think a particular way, than the rule of law has no meaning and our society is reduced to racial and gender warfare where the winning side can impose apartheid in order to assure that their view of the law prevails.

Nominating a judicial nominee is a political game, but judging is not. President Obama, and all future presidents, would do well to refrain from politicalizing the judiciary by politicalizing the nomination process.

A WISE JURIST

(May 27, 2009)

Yesterday President Obama nominated Judge Sonia Sotomayor to the Supreme Court to replace retiring Justice David Souter. In announcing his nominee, Obama described her as not only having a distinguished legal career, but also as having an "inspiring" life story that, presumably, gives her greater empathy. It has been reported that the selection of Sotomayor was made on the basis of identity politics—calculating that nominating a Hispanic to the Court "would energize a key and growing constituency."

Liberal commentators predict with glee that the Republicans will lose the Hispanic vote if they challenge the "first" Hispanic appointee to the Supreme Court. As an initial matter, it should be noted that Justice Benjamin Cardoza was, technically, the first Hispanic to serve on the high court.

Secondly, do Democrats really think so little of Hispanics that they will equate attacking a nominee on her judicial philosophy as the same thing as attacking her on her ethnicity (or gender)? Such belittlingly the intelligence of an entire racial group is blatant discrimination. It is unfortunate that the President who once said that there is "no black

America, no white America" can only see the color of one's skin rather than the merit of one's character.

Finally, there is dubious support for the proposition that the electorate cares about the race or gender of judicial appointees. For instance, did President Reagan gain any women votes in his re-election bid for having appointed the first female justice? Or did Democrats suffer at the polls for filibustering President George W. Bush's nomination of Migueal Estrada to serve on the D.C. Circuit Court of Appeals?

The disturbing aspect of this nomination, however, is the overt racism of the president in playing the race card. In announcing his nominee, Obama made a point to emphasis Sotomayor's ethnicity and noticeably rolled his "r's" when stating that her parents came from Puerrrto Rrrrico. New York Senator Charles Schumer bluntly stated, "It's long overdue that a Latino sit on the United States Supreme Court." As has already been discussed, affirmative action for the judiciary is not only racist, but reduces the rule of law to packing the court with the race or gender of the month.

But it is one thing to politicize the nomination process by playing racial politics, it is quite another for such a philosophy to actually be embraced by the nominee. But that is exactly what Sotomayor's public statements reveal—a judge who sees the law not through the lenses of blind justice but through the prism of race and gender.

In a 2001 lecture at the University of California (Berkeley) School of Law, Sotomayor argued, after first disputing that there is such a thing as wisdom, that "I would hope that a wise Latina woman with the richness of her experiences would more often than not reach a better conclusion than a white male who hasn't lived that life." Reverend Jeremiah Wright, President Obama's long-time pastor, couldn't have said it better himself.

In other portions of the speech, which was published in 2002 in the Berkeley Law Raza ("The Race") Law Journal, Sotomayor stated that, "Our experiences as women and people of color affect our decisions. The aspiration to impartiality is just that—it's an aspiration because it denies the fact that we are by our experiences making different choices than others..." In other words, there can be no such thing as equal protection under the law because a color-blind society is an unattainable aspiration.

Later in the speech she states that, "Whether born from experience or inherent physiological or cultural differences, a possibility I abhor less or discount less..., our gender and national origins may and will make a difference in our judging." Judging impartially is not simply an aspiration, but Sotomayor appears to be open to the argument that such an aspiration is an impossibility because we can no more rise above our "inherent physiological or cultural differences" than change our skin color. Racial conflict is the natural and inescapable outcome of such a philosophy.

Any white male who made similar statements in a magazine called The Master Race would be denounced as a bigot and shunned from any role in our legal or political institutions. But such racism from a minority has become so acceptable to the mainstream media that they barely raise an eyebrow at such comments or at a nomination obviously made to play the race card.

Sotomayor, who rejoices in "how wonderful and magical it is to have a Latina soul" and who applauds "being a Latina voice on the bench," should remember Judge Learned Hand's eulogy for Justice Benjamin Cardozo in 1938:

> The wise man is the detached man. Our convictions, our outlook, the whole makeup of our thinking, which we cannot

> help bringing to the decision of every question, is the creature of our past; and into our past have been woven all sorts of frustrated ambitions with their envies, and of hopes of preferment with their corruptions, which, long since forgotten, determine our conclusions. A wise man is one exempt from the handicap of such a past; he is a runner stripped for the race; he can weigh the conflicting factors from his problem without always finding himself in one scale or the other.

Contrary to a judicial philosophy of empathy in which a jurist "throws the game" for his favorite side, the wise judge is the one who is able to remove himself from the case before him and to render judgment based on the merits alone. Justice is not served by a judge identifying with people's hopes and struggles (Obama's definition of empathy), but by a jurist following the law regardless of personal sympathies.

ADVICE AND CONSENT

(May 31, 2009)

In the coming months the Senate will hold confirmation hearings on President Obama's nomination of Judge Sotomayor to replace Justice David Souter on the U.S. Supreme Court. In the past week since the nomination was announced, there has been much debate over what the tone and tenor of the confirmation hearings should be. The president has called for an end to partisan debates over judicial nominees, and the administration has warned Republicans that attacking the "first" Hispanic nominee to the Supreme Court would cost them Hispanic votes.

The Republican Party appears split on what course they should take at the hearings. Most GOP senators, apparently believing that the possibility of alienating the Hispanic vote is not worth the risk of opposing the nomination of a liberal to replace a liberal, have merely expressed tepid opposition to Sotomayor. Others within the party, however, have urged GOP senators to take a more vigorous stand against Sotomayor based on her views of empathy, identity jurisprudence and reverse discrimination, gun control, homosexual marriage, etc.

Under the Constitution, the president has the power to appoint judges to the federal courts with the "advice and consent of the Senate." What does "advice and consent" mean in the context of judicial confirmation hearings? Should senators simply inquire into the intellectual and ethical qualifications of the nominee and, if those are met, rubber stamp the appointment to the Supreme Court? Or is the nominee's ideology and stance on such issues as abortion, homosexual marriage, and religious liberty fair game?

In answering this question, it should first be noted that President Obama has invited a more thorough examination of his nominee by touting her "inspiring" life story and claiming that she shares his views on judicial empathy. If President Obama nominated her because he believed her life experiences would enable her to identify with the hopes and struggles of the "victims" before her (i.e., "poor, or African American, or gay..."), than senators have every right to examine her life and her sympathizes to determine exactly how they will translate into her rulings from the bench.

In every confirmation hearing, however, it is imperative that senators examine the ideology of the nominee. For if the Constitution is the supreme law of the land and the guardian of our rights and liberties, its integrity demands that senators inquire into how a particular nominee will interpret it. If the nominee has a goal-oriented or "victim"-oriented jurisprudence and believes in rights not found in the document (the right of privacy, for instance), that nominee should be opposed by all available means—up to and including filibuster. Nor is rejecting a nominee based on ideological grounds new, for George Washington's nomination of John Rutledge in 1795 and President Polk's nomination of George Woodward in 1845 were defeated on ideological grounds.

President Obama clearly understands that the Senate's role in confirmation hearings is not to simply rubber-stamp a president's nominee. On Meet the Press in October 2006, he stated that it is acceptable not to vote for a nominee "because you're not sure that their views on the Constitution comport with yours." He even joined the (unsuccessful) Democratic effort to block Judge Samuel Alito's confirmation to the Supreme Court in 2006 with a filibuster, arguing that, even though "I have no doubt that Judge Alito has the training and qualifications necessary to serve," he was "deeply troubled" because as a federal judge Alito "constantly side[d] on behalf of the powerful against the powerless; on behalf of a strong government or corporation against upholding American's individual rights."

That is what this debate is all about—the Democrats attempt to pack the federal judiciary with judges who will rule for Democratic causes when they cannot win at the polls. That is why, just forty-five minutes after President Reagan nominated Judge Robert Bork to the Supreme Court in 1987, Senator Ted Kennedy took to the Senate floor and lambasted what he called "Robert Bork's America." That is why in 1991 Senate Democrats put Judge Clarence Thomas through a "high-tech lynching" when he was nominated to the high court by President George H.W. Bush.

That is why Senate Democrats filibustered President George W. Bush's nomination of Miguel Estrada to the D.C. Circuit Court of Appeals in 2001, and why in 2006 they did the same thing with Judge Janice Rogers Brown in 2005. At that time, Senator Pat Leahy stated that he opposed voting for Judge Brown because she would rule against "working men and women and families across the Nation."

It is only by engaging in the "politicalization" of the judicial nomination process that was begun by Democrats can we hope to prevent the politicalization of the courts. The battle is for the very meaning of the Constitution and the soul of the judiciary. Both sides have understood this for decades, but so far only the Democrats have actually waged the battle. If Republicans don't join the fray, the battle for the Constitution will be lost and judges will be free to legislate from the bench. It is time to take the gloves off.

AMENDING UNALIENABLE RIGHTS

(May 31, 2009)

In an editorial on May 29th entitled "Gay-marriage ruling less than it appears," The Des Moines Register argued that, in effect, We the People cannot change our constitution via the amendment process to reverse an earlier court ruling. Last week the California Supreme Court held that Proposition 8, passed by a majority of voters in 2008, was in fact constitutional. Prop 8 amended the California Constitution to declare that only heterosexual marriage is valid in that state, overruling an earlier ruling by the California Supreme Court which held that gays had a right to marry.

The Register, however, argues that the California Supreme Court limited the amendment in such a way as to avoid changing it's "earlier holding that gay couples cannot be denied the same constitutional rights that heterosexual couples enjoy." The Register hypothesizes that, if the court did not limit the amendment's reading, it "likely would have struck down the amendment entirely because it would have violated the equal-protection clause of...the state...constitution[]" as previously interpreted by that court.

Stating that "this line of reasoning has implications for Iowa," the Register argues that, if the Iowa Constitution were amended to prohibit homosexual marriage, the Iowa Supreme Court would strike it down as unconstitutional because "[a]n amendment that would strip same-sex couples of [marriage] rights could not be squared with [the court's] earlier ruling."

Among the many problems with the Register's analysis of the California Supreme Court's ruling is that the Court explicitly rejected the argument made by the Register. In its opinion, the court ruled:

> [T]he Attorney General maintains that "Proposition 8 should be invalidated even if it is deemed to amend the Constitution because it abrogates fundamental rights

protected by article 1 without a compelling interest."...

[But] the "inalienable" nature of a constitutional right never has been understood to preclude the adoption of a constitutional amendment that limits or restricts the scope or application of such a right....

Accordingly, there is no basis for suggesting that the inalienable rights set forth in article 1, section 1, and the other provisions of the Declaration of Rights, are of a higher order than —and thus exempt from—the people's right to "alter or reform" the Constitution through either the legislative or the initiative constitutional amendment process. Indeed, a review of the current version of the constitutional provisions contained within article 1's Declaration of Rights demonstrates that modification

> of such rights through the amendment process has occurred throughout our state's history. (The emphasis in original.)

It is bad enough that the Register ignored the court's rejection of its argument, but the Register perpetuated its wrong by misconstruing the court's opinion to the people of Iowa in such a way as to support the opposite of what it said. So much for journalistic, or editorial, integrity.

Furthermore, the Register's argument reveals a fundamental misunderstanding of the nature of our constitutional democracy. The supreme law of the land is not simply the Constitution, but the will of the people as embodied in the Constitution. We the People are the creators of our Constitution, and we established in that document the procedures whereby we can amend or alter that document as we see fit.

If the people choose to exercise their right to amend their constitution, the courts are powerless to stop them. As the California Supreme Court noted in its ruling, to do otherwise "would exceed the well-established and time-honored limits of the judicial role were we to take it upon ourselves to fashion such a restriction upon the present and future right of the people to determine the content of the Constitution that governs our state."

As the court noted, several well-respected commentators concur that We the People are our own rulers. Liberal constitutional thinker Lawrence Tribe wrote, "allowing the judiciary to pass on the merits of constitutional amendments would unequivocally subordinate the amendment process to the legal system it is intended to override and would thus gravely threaten the integrity of the entire structure." Another commentator argued, "To empower the courts not simply to review the procedures whereby amendments were adopted but also to void amendments on the basis of their substantive content would surely threaten the notion of a government founded on the consent of the governed."

Finally, the Register's argument is wrong in practice, as both the 11th, 13th, 14th, and 15th Amendments were passed in direct response to Supreme Court decisions that the American people felt were wrongly decided. In fact, the 13th Amendment took away "inalienable property rights" of slave owners that were estimated at a total value of $1,576,206,000 (not adjusted for inflation).

Contrary to what The Des Moines Register may say about its ruling, the California Supreme Court's opinion clearly holds that We the People may amend our fundamental will as reflected in the Constitution in any way we so choose, and no court may stop us. And if they should try, they should be impeached. And any editorial board that advocates such a position under the guise of knowingly misconstruing a court decision should be thrown out.

IDENTITY JURISPRUDENCE
(April 14, 2010)

As the media continues to speculate over who President Obama will appoint to replace Justice John Paul Stevens on the Supreme Court, one thing is abundantly clear—their obsession with identity politics. Liberal constituencies have put together their wish list of "firsts" for the nominee: the first black female justice, the first gay justice, or the first Native American justice among other possible firsts.

The Obama White House has shown that the identity of its nominees is almost as important as their ideology. According to Brookings Institution's Russell Wheeler, Obama's nominees have "included proportionately fewer white men, slightly more Hispanics, substantially more African-Americans and

Asian-Americans, and more sitting judges" than his predecessor did.

But President Bush was not immune to engaging in affirmative action for the judiciary. Bush, bowing to the intense pressure to nominate a female to replace the retiring Justice Sandra Day O'Connor, the first woman to sit on the Supreme Court, nominated Harriet Miers, a nomination which went from bad to worse and which was later withdrawn.

Underlying this obsession with identity politics, however, is the insidious and prejudiced belief that all people of a specific gender or race think alike and would rule on cases in the same way. Rather than looking solely at the merit of a particular nominee, proponents of affirmative action for the federal bench would categorize nominees by their gender and race and thereby presume to know how they would vote on particular cases.

Women are presumed to vote to uphold Roe v. Wade, blacks are assumed to support the liberal civil rights agenda (including affirmative action), and a wise Latina woman, "in the richness of her experiences[,] would more often than not reach a better conclusion than a white male." Given this, I suppose the ideal "master race" for a justice would be a transgender of mixed racial-minority background.

And last, but not least, white men are presumed to be narrow-minded Neanderthals who are for big business and big government against the little guy.

But not only do identity politics categorize nominees by gender and race in violation of equal protection, it transforms the law itself from blind, neutral justice to a matter of genetics. Though while those who indulge in identity politics do so in the name of diversity, they too often speak only in terms of race or gender—rather than one's economic, social, and educational background—as the reason they would bring a diverse perspective to the table.

The logical conclusion of a racial/gender wish lists for judicial nominees is that one's genetic makeup predestines one's ideology. But as Justice Antonin Scalia noted in an interview on CNBC shortly after O'Connor's retirement, "as far as the product of the court is concerned, [a female replacement] makes no difference at all. I don't think there's...a female legal answer to a question and a male legal answer to the same question. That's just silly."

The law should mean the same thing, regardless of the gender or race of the particular judge before which the case is heard. If it doesn't, then the law can be manipulated by simply court-packing the federal bench with gender or racial clones who all think a particular way.

The logical consequences of identity politics lead to only two options—apartheid or genocide. For if our morals, values, and ideology are preordained by our genetics, we must either live under an apartheid system, whereby each would live with their own kind in separate communities according to their own rules, or the law is then reduced to racial and gender warfare in which the winner takes all.

Identity politics is nothing more than blatant group-based discrimination, and it is only by refusing to play this game that we can fulfill Dr. Martin Luther King's dream of "a nation where [we] will not be judged by the color of [our] skin but by [our] character."

Eight Questions for Bob Vander Plaats
(May 8, 2010)

Judicial activism was brought home to Iowans last April when the Iowa Supreme Court struck down the state's Defense of Marriage Act (DOMA), leading to a debate, lively at times, over what the conservative response should be. At its core, this discussion is over what the law is, who decides it, and, more recently, what should happen if the law is immoral.

One of the Republican candidates for governor, Bob Vander Plaats, and those who support him (in particular, the Iowa Family Policy Center (IFPC), WHO Radio's Steve Deace, and Bill Salier, the co-founder of Everyday America) have argued that the court's ruling does not have to be enforced.

Their position is based on the postulation, which they have taken great pains to repeat over and over again, that the courts cannot make law but only issue advisory opinions. Vander Plaats, appearing on Deace's radio show May 12th, stated that, "the legislature makes the law, the executive branch executes the law, the people get to amend the Constitution, and the court gets to offer opinion."

Sailer, appearing at a rally with Vander Plaats shortly after the Court issued its decision, said that lawmakers needed to thank the justices for their opinion, but tell them that it's merely their opinion and that DOMA is still on the books.

He continued: "[Lawmakers] can face down the court and say, 'We passed DOMA, the Defense of Marriage Act. You claim that it is stricken. And yet unless some magic eraser came down from the sky, it's still in code.'" Because DOMA is still on the books, they argue that the governor, as the state's "chief magistrate," should continue to enforce it.

Assuming, arguendo, that they are correct, this theory raises several important questions which neither Vander Plaats nor his supporters have ever provided specific answers. These questions are not a personal attack on Vander Plaats or his supporters, but are an honest attempt to understand what it is they do, or do not, believe.

Any theory of law and governance does not revolve around just one case and one governor, but has to account for its application in other cases as well. This isn't just a debate over judicially ordered gay marriage, but has ramifications for our entire understanding of government.

Vander Plaats himself has indicated that he understands this when he stated at a house party last fall that, "[t]he reason why you need a governor to issue the executive order goes way beyond marriage. If you continue to allow a Supreme Court to drive a car without a license, every one of your freedoms is up for grabs. Private property. Free enterprise. Freedom of speech. Freedom of religion. Freedom of assembly."

If Vander Plaats wants us to vote for him and support his theory, than he needs to explain how he will implement it across the board.

Question #1: Why Do We Need an Executive "Stay?" Vander Plaats has promised that, immediately upon taking the oath of office, he will issue an executive order that will, temporarily at least, "stay" the court's opinion. But why, if the court can only issue opinions and not make law, does the opinion have to be stayed? Opinions don't need to be stayed; only laws do.

Bryan English, spokesman for the IFPC, appeared to agree that an executive "stay" is unnecessary when he was a guest on Deace's afternoon radio show on May 5th. In making his point that the courts have no power to enforce their own decisions, he referred to a question he had earlier posed to Terry Branstad: "Who was going to get down off their bench over there at the Supreme Court and come force a governor to treat their opinion as if it were law?"

Why should Vander Plaats, or any other governor, issue an executive "stay" and thereby recognize the validity of the court's decision, acknowledge that it has the force of law, but then assume the power to stay the force of that law? An executive "stay" implies that the Court's ruling is enforceable, but that it will be "paused" momentarily before it resumes the force of law.

Vander Plaats seemed to acknowledge this when, in a recent meeting with the Sioux City Journal's editorial board, he referred to this executive "stay" as the "proverbial timeout." As a candidate for governor, Vander Plaats owes Iowans an explanation as to why an executive "stay" is necessary under his theory.

Question #2: Why Does the Legislature Need to Act? Vander Plaats and his supporters argue that such a "stay" would be temporary until the people of Iowa and/or their legislature responded to the court's opinion. But, again, why would the legislature need to act at all if DOMA is still good law, regardless of what the court thinks? Why, in the words of both Vander Plaats and Bryan English, did the court's advisory opinion put the "onus" back on the legislature?

Does the legislature have to reenact DOMA for it to remain good law even though, as the theory goes, it is supposedly still good law? Do they need to pass a constitutional DOMA amendment even though, again, DOMA itself remains good law? As a candidate for governor, Vander Plaats owes Iowans an explanation as to why the legislature would need to reenact supposedly good law, and whether a constitutional DOMA amendment is really necessary.

Question #3: What is the Extent of the Executive Power to "Stay" something? Vander Plaats and his supporters have argued that this "stay" will stop gay marriage licenses from being issue in this state until the legislature acts. But marriage licenses are issued by local county recorders who, traditionally, are not members of the Executive Branch. Does Vander Plaats believe he has the authority to order local officials to refuse to issue gay marriage licenses?

Vander Plaats has also failed to explain how long this unnecessary executive "stay" would last while the legislature reenacts legislation that is already good law. Will it be in effect for only the 2011-2012 General Assembly and then lapse if a constitutional DOMA amendment does not pass out of the legislature? Or could it possibly remain in force for a longer period of time? Could it remain in effect indefinitely?

What historical practice would Vander Plaats rely upon in determining the length of his "stay?" And could legislative silence ever, in and of itself, constitute a legislative response to the court's opinion? Isn't doing nothing as good a response as doing something?

Can the governor also issue a "stay" against laws enacted by the legislature? On Deace's radio show on May 12th, Vander Plaats seemed to indicate that the "stay" would remain in effect until the legislature and/or the people made sure God's law that marriage is between one man and one woman was the law in Iowa.

Does this mean that, even if the people and/or their legislators decided to pass legislation or a constitutional amendment allowing for gay marriage, Vander Plaats would issue an executive "stay" against that as well because it violates God's law? As a candidate for governor, Vander Plaats owes Iowans an explanation as to how long his executive "stay" would last, and if he would "stay" legislation/ constitutional amendments.

Question #4: Are All Court Decisions Merely Advisory? As already noted, Vander Plaats and his supporters have argued that courts cannot make law but only issue opinions. However, on Deace's June 25, 2009 show, both he and Vander Plaats seemed to agree that the Court could issue a binding opinion, based on the Constitution, that former Governor Vislack could not issue an executive order reinstating the voting rights of felons. Why can the Court issue a legally binding decision in one case and not the other?

This leads to the larger question of which court decisions are merely advisory and which ones are binding? Are only court decisions which rule something unconstitutional advisory, or are all court decisions advisory? Bryan English, appearing on Deace's May 5th radio show, seemed to indicate that the theory would encompass all court decisions when he argued that the state should have refused to obey a 1993 Iowa Supreme Court decision, based on Iowa law rather than the Constitution, that told the State to increase public employees' pay.

Steve Deace and his guest David Barton of Wallbuilders echoed these sentiments on Deace's show on May 7th. But if all court decisions are merely advisory without the force of law, then criminal convictions, divorce proceedings, contracts, and wills/trusts would be unenforceable.

If, on the other hand, court decisions are merely advisory only when they determine something is unconstitutional, is it limited to legislative acts or does it include executive orders, local ordinances, administrative regulations, and police practices/ policies? If Vander Plaats does make a distinction between which court decisions are or are not advisory opinions, what historical practice does he rely upon?

If court decisions are advisory, why would Vander Plaats support a legal challenge to ObamaCare? Isn't such a lawsuit a waste of time and money if President Obama is free to tell the courts "thanks but no thanks" for their opinion? What justification would he provide from challenging federal health care or any other law he deems is unconstitutional?

Also, if court decisions are merely advisory, why should we bother to criticize them? If they are just musings by a bunch of old, robed individuals, why should we care? Why not let them think what they want and we'll do what we want? Why should we care about judicial nominees? As a candidate for governor, Vander Plaats owes Iowans an explanation as to whether all, or only some, court rulings are merely advisory and the reasons why.

Question #5: What Other Court Decisions Would Not Be Enforced? Vander Plaats cites the governor's role as "chief magistrate" for his authority to enforce the laws on the books, regardless of whether the courts rule them unconstitutional. If this is true, than certainly the "chief magistrate" of a state has the authority to ignore mere advisory opinions issued by either federal or state courts because, in both cases, the state laws remain on the books as good law.

Would, for instance, Vander Plaats reintroduce Prison Fellowship Ministry's rehabilitation program back into Iowa prisons even though the 8th Circuit held it to be unconstitutional? Would he allow prayer back in public school classrooms? Would he plant a set of marble Ten Commandments in front of the governor's mansion at Terrance Hill?

Would he rule that illegal immigrants born in this country do not have birthright citizenship, a position which he hinted at when he was interviewed by Deace on June 25, 2009? Would he deny illegal immigrants a free public education? Would he prohibit access to pornography? As a candidate for governor, Vander Plaats owes Iowans an explanation as to which court decisions he would "stay" and those he would enforce and the reasons for each.

Question #6: Who Else Can Ignore Court Decisions? Last spring, Vander Plaats and his supporters had urged county recorders to refuse to issue marriage licenses to same-sex couples. Does this mean that Vander Plaats believes that other officials, and not just the "chief magistrate" of the state, have the ability, if not the duty, to ignore mere court opinions?

If so, which officials can and cannot do so? Does it only apply to elected officials (county sheriff, county attorneys, etc.), or does it apply to non-elected officials such as city managers and police chiefs? Does it apply to mere state/local rank-and-file employees, or only department/agency heads?

Does it apply to individuals as well, and does it matter if they are citizens, lawful alien residents, or illegal immigrants? As a candidate for governor, Vander Plaats owes Iowans an explanation as to who can or cannot refuse to obey a court opinion.

Question #7: What Should Be Done to Those Who Obey the Court's Opinion? As previously mentioned, Vander Plaats and his supporters maintain that a court cannot make law and, therefore, laws remain in effect until the legislature changes them. This naturally begs the question of what, if anything, should be done to those individuals, whether the "chief magistrate" or another official, who executes the court's decision in violation of the existing law which, again, is still good law?

Should they be impeached and removed from office? Should criminal proceedings be instituted against them? On Steve Deace's May 5th radio show, both he and Bryan English indicated that a governor could be impeached for following a court order rather than the law on the books.

On June 4th of last year, Deace and his guests referred to those "chief magistrates" who obeyed court decisions as acting "illegally, unilaterally, and unconstitutionally," and they called for all officials who refused to follow the duly enacted law to be, at a minimum, removed from office. As a candidate for governor, Vander Plaats owes Iowans an explanation as to what, according to his theory, should be done to those who, in essence, commit treason.

Question #8: Can a Governor Refuse to Execute an Immoral Law? Vander Plaats and his supporters have called out Rod Roberts for saying that, if the voters rejected a constitutional DOMA amendment, he would consider himself morally bound to enforce same-sex marriage in the state.

Steve Deace appeared to say that a Christian's allegiance to God's law overrides his obligations as an elected official when, on his May 5th show, he exalted the example of Christians who refused to say "Caesar is Lord." On Deace's May 12th radio show, Vander Plaats stated that "the law comes from God... the Lawgiver. All laws originate from the Lawgiver."

He went on to argue that, "[i]f a law contradicts the law of God, than it is incongruent...If we understand what is the basis and origin of all law, and if it doesn't match up, if it doesn't square, if it doesn't meet the plum line of the law of God, than I believe with Martin Luther King that [it] is not a law. All of a sudden it's a made-up law. And we as a people then need to take a stand. And we need to take a stand for God's law."

Would he agree to enforce same-sex marriage in Iowa if the people rejected a constitutional amendment, or would he be unable to do so because it would be immoral? Does he believe that immoral laws are void from conception, and thus he could act as if they were never on the books? Would God's moral law compel him to enact by executive fiat certain laws?

Would he, for instance, issue an executive order prohibiting gambling in the state? Would he shut down abortion clinics? Would he order businesses closed on the Sabbath? Would he enforce prohibition? What other laws would he not enforce because he thinks they are immoral? As a candidate for governor, Vander Plaats owes Iowans an explanation as to how his moral code affects what laws he will enforce, and which ones he feels compelled to order without legislative authority.

In conclusion, this debate isn't just about one single court case and what should be done about it, but it involves fundamental principles about how our secular, constitutional republic is supposed to function. The onus is on Vander Plaats to be able to adequately explain his theory and its implications, and until he does, he gives the people of Iowa no reason to be confident that he understands that our government is one of laws and not of men or ayatollahs.

IS PRIOR JUDICIAL EXPERIENCE NECESSARY?

(May 10, 2010)

This past Monday President Obama nominated Solicitor General Elena Kagan to replace retiring Justice John Paul Stevens on the United States Supreme Court. As Solicitor General, a position she has held since being confirmed by the Senate on a 61-31 vote in March 2009, Kagan serves as the federal government's primary advocate before the Supreme Court. Previously, Kagan served as dean of Harvard Law School, a professor at the University of Chicago Law School, and as an attorney in the Clinton Department of Justice.

Despite her pedigree, the one thing Kagan has never been is a judge at either the state or local level. Ironically, Kagan herself, in a law review article entitled Confirmation Messes, Old and New, appeared to indicate that prior judicial experience was necessary to ensure that a nominee have the "previous accomplishments" and "training" to not just "handle but to master the 'craft' aspects of being a judge."

Every single member of the current Court, including outgoing Justice Stevens, has had prior experience as a federal appellate judge, a job requirement that recent polls have found that 70 percent of the public say they want in a nominee. Justices William H. Rehnquist and Lewis F. Powell, Jr. were the last justices nominated who had no prior judicial service.

This "requirement" of prior judicial experience, however, is a modern development of the past quarter century. Historically, most Supreme Court nominees were private attorneys, high-ranking administration officials, and/or politicians without prior judicial experience. Notable examples just among chief justices include Earl Warren, Charles Evan Hughes, Salmon Chase, Roger Taney, and John Marshall.

Though prior judicial experience is not necessary to make someone a Supreme Court justice, it is increasingly necessary to provide a paper trail by which the Senate, and the American people, can judge a nominee's understanding of the Constitution. The real requirement is not whether a nominee has previously donned a black robe, but whether he or she has demonstrated in past statements, whether on or off the bench, a proper understanding of the role of judges in our constitutional republic.

This, and not prior judicial experience, is the one qualification for the Court that Kagan lacks, and because of it, as Senator Grassley noted, "[t]he Judiciary Committee must take time to ensure that the nominee will be true to the Constitution and apply the law, not personal politics, feelings or preferences. With no judicial experience, it becomes even more important that we ask thorough questions to determine that Ms. Kagan truly understands the constitutional role of a Supreme Court justice."

Kagan herself understands that, in this battle over the meaning of the Constitution and judicial activism, nothing is off limits. In her law review article discussing confirmation hearings, she astutely writes:

The problem is not that the Senate focused too much on a nominee's legal views, but that it did so far too little....The kind of inquiry that would contribute most to understanding and evaluating a nomination is ... discussion first, of the nominee's broad judicial philosophy and, second, of her views on particular constitutional issues....

Hence the second aspect of the inquiry: the insistence on seeing how theory works in practice by evoking a nominee's comments on particular issues—involving privacy rights, free speech, race and gender discrimination, and so forth—that the Court regularly faces.

[As for claims that such inquiry would compromise "judicial independence":] The judicial independence that we should focus on protecting resides primarily in the inability

> of political officials, once having placed a person on the court, to interfere with what she does there. That seems a fair amount of independence for any branch of government.
>
> [W]hat is worse even than the hearings themselves is … the evident belief of many senators that serious substantive inquiry of nominees is usually not only inessential, but illegitimate.

Kagan may enter the confirmation hearings with a clean slate free of any paper trail, but senators must not let her leave the same way she came in. By her own admission, everything is fair game, and it is essential and perfectly legitimate for senators to learn her position on every issue that may come before the court.

DISPELLING FIVE MYTHS ABOUT JUDICIAL REVIEW (May 19, 2010)

In the ongoing debate over the response to the Iowa Supreme Court's decision to strike down the state's Defense of Marriage Act, there are several persistent myths over the doctrine of judicial review that have cropped up and found a voice in Iowa. Proponents of these myths hope to be able to reign in judicial activism by removing the power of courts to "make law."

The first and most prominent among these myths is the claim that the power of judicial review can be found no where in the text of the Constitution. All the Constitution provides is that "[t] he judicial Power of the United States, shall be vested in one Supreme Court.."

But long before Chief Justice John Marshall famously expounded on the subject in Marbury v. Madison (1803), those who wrote and ratified the Constitution understood the term "judicial power" in the text to encompass the power of judicial review. At the Constitutional Convention, Luther Martin stated that "as to the Constitutionality of laws, that point will come before the Judges in their proper official character. In this character they have a negative on the laws."

George Mason also noted that "in their expository capacity as Judges…[t]hey could declare an unconstitutional law void." James Madison stated that a "law violating a constitution established by the people themselves, would be considered by the Judges as null & void."

Patrick Henry argued during the Virginia ratifying convention that "I take it as the highest encomium of this country, that the acts of the legislature, if unconstitutional, are liable to be opposed by the judiciary."

Thomas Jefferson, in a letter to James Madison in which he argued for a Bill of Rights, declared: "In the arguments in favor of a declaration of rights, you omit one which has great weight with me, the legal check which it puts into the hands of the judiciary." (It wasn't until the Supreme Court began to disagree with him, nearly fifteen years after the Constitution was ratified, that Jefferson's opinion of judicial review began to change.)

These are just a few of the statements made by our Founders that show that they clearly understood that the term "judicial power" encompassed the power of judicial review. It is also important to note that, though several did express dissatisfaction with the power of judicial review, no one during the Constitutional Convention or the ratifying debates claimed that the judiciary did not possess such a power.

The second myth is that, even if the courts have the power to declare a law unconstitutional, they cannot enforce their decision but only state their opinion. But James Madison stated at the Constitutional Convention that laws would be "set aside by the National Tribunals." (emphasis added) Gouveneur Morris also used this active term when he expressed the belief that a "law which ought to be negatived will be set aside in the Judiciary department."

In addition, at the Maryland ratifying convention, Luther Martin stated that: "Whether, therefore, any laws or regulations of the Congress, any acts of its President or other officers, are contrary to, or not warranted by, the Constitution, rests only with the judges, who are appointed by Congress, to determine; by whose determinations every state must be bound." (emphasis added)

John Jay, writing in Federalist No. 64, wrote "that the judgments of our courts...are as valid and as binding on all persons whom they concern, as the laws passed by our legislature. All constitutional acts of power, whether in the executive or in the judicial department, have as much legal validity and obligation as if they proceeded from the legislature..."

Brutus, writing in The Anti-Federalist Papers No. 78-79, feared that the Supreme Court would, because of the doctrine of judicial review, be "superior to that of the legislature." In fact, he specifically contrasted this American understanding of judicial review with that in England in which Parliament can set aside or correct, via legislation, the opinions of their courts.

The power to set aside an unconstitutional law, or parts thereof, is essential to the power of judicial review, for without it they are but a resounding gong. If courts are unable to enforce their determination that a law is unconstitutional, than they cannot serve as the "legal check" Jefferson had in mind, or as the "guardian of those [bill of] rights" Madison talked about in the 1st session of Congress.

There is not a single quote among any of the Founding Generation that supports the proposition that, once a court rules a law is unconstitutional, the law remains the law until the legislature opts to change it. Before Marbury, American courts had declared several laws unconstitutional, both before and after the Constitution, and no one questioned the legal force of those decisions.

Also, there is not a single example of a "chief magistrate"—whether Jefferson, Jackson, or Lincoln—who issued an executive "stay" or even contemplated one. (The Emancipation Proclamation was a military order intended to deprive the South of the slave labor that worked the farms, freeing their owners to serve in the Confederate Army. It only had effect in enemy territory, and Lincoln never imagined he had the authority to issue it nationwide as a "stay" on the Court's Dred Scott (1857) decision.)

The third myth is that judicial review equals judicial law making. A judicial veto of an unconstitutional piece of legislation is not the same as the power to order the legislature and executive branches to enact legislation. Just as no one claims that a President is "making law" by exercising his constitutionally-delegated veto power, the same holds true for a judicial veto. Removing unconstitutional portions of a law from the books is not the same as adding law to the code.

The fourth myth is that judicial review would make the judiciary supreme to the other branches of government. In Federalist #78, Alexander Hamilton rejected this proposition in the following passage:

Nor does this conclusion by any means suppose a superiority of the judicial to the legislative power. It only supposes that the power of the people is superior to both, and that where the will of the legislature, declared in its statutes, stands in opposition to that of the people, declared in the

Constitution, the judges ought to be governed by the later rather than the former.

In other words, the judiciary is not supreme over the other two branches, but the Constitution is supreme over all three. Simply because the judiciary is the last to have a chance to declare a law unconstitutional doesn't mean it is supreme. The legislature can always elect not to pass a law because they believe it is unconstitutional, or the executive can always veto a piece of legislation because he believes it is unconstitutional. All three co-equal branches of government have to concur before a law passes constitutional muster.

The fifth and final myth of judicial review is that, if it weren't for the courts, we wouldn't have a liberal agenda pushed down our throats. Thanks to the courts, as the theory goes, we have abortion, homosexual marriage, flag burning, birthright citizenship for illegals, unfettered access to pornography, the removal of prayer from the public schools, etc.

There are three problems with this myth. The first is—so what? Just because we don't like the result doesn't mean the courts do not have the power. In fact, stressing this point only makes it appear that this position is taken not on constitutional principle but on disgust with liberal judges.

The second is that the other branches, at both the local, state, and federal levels, deserve much of the blame for the liberal agenda in our country—the indoctrination of liberalism in our public education, ObamaCare, environmental regulations, strict gun laws, taking of private property through eminent domain and economic regulation, etc.

The third problem is that the courts have occasionally gotten the law right, including such cases as Citizens United v. FEC (2010) (campaign finance), Brown v. Board of Education (1954) (desegregation), U.S. v. Lopez (1995) (federalism), Good News Club v. Milford Central (2001) (equal access to school property for religious clubs), and D.C. v. Heller (2008) (gun rights). One cannot argue that the cases the court got wrong are not binding but the ones it got right are. Either both are binding, or both are not.

In conclusion, there is nothing unconstitutional about the power of judicial review. There are legitimate remedies to the abuses of that power, but trying to discredit its existence is not one of them.

JUDGING JUDGES

(June 10, 2010)

Now that the primaries are finally over, Iowans can turn their attention to the general election in November in which they will decide not only which candidates to elect, but also which judges should be retained and whether or not the state should hold a constitutional convention.

Unlike states that have judicial elections, Iowa has adopted the "Missouri Plan" in which nominating committees pick the names of two (or, in the case of appellate courts, three) candidates out of a pool of applicants to send to the governor, who then selects one to fill the vacancy.

After one year in office, and then at varying intervals thereafter depending on the type of judicial office held, judges stand for a retention vote. They do not face any challengers on the ballot. Rather, voters are simply asked whether or not a particular judge should keep their job based on their performance.

Of the unanimous Iowa Supreme Court that struck down the state's DOMA statute last year, three of the justices stand for a retention vote this November: Chief Justice Marsha Ternus and Justices Michael Streit and David Baker.

In the final GOP gubernatorial debate during the primary, two of the contenders, both of whom eventually lost, stated that they would urge Iowans not to retain these justices. They were criticized for this by some in the media, who argued that "voters, in retention elections, may [only] remove judges for cause (such as malfeasance)—not for rulings that are unpopular."

There is nothing, however, in the language on the ballot itself or in the Iowa Constitution or the Iowa Code that prevents voters from removing judges for any other reason than "cause." The Iowa Constitution limits the use of impeachment to "any misdemeanor or malfeasance in office," but there is no such limitation on the ability of voters to refuse to retain judges at the ballot box.

These media critics are right to be concerned that the threat of a campaign to unseat a judge may undermine the judicial independence necessary for that branch to enforce constitutional limits on the other two branches. Prudence, therefore, would caution that this option be reserved for those cases in which a judge (or judges) clearly engaged in judicial activism. Judicial activism is an oft-used, but rarely defined, term thrown about by those on both sides of the ideological spectrum to label decisions that they don't agree with.

But for a constitutionalist, judicial activism is defined by a clear departure from the original understanding of the words of the Constitution. Certainly those guided by such original understanding do not always agree among themselves in every case, but originalism provides the perimeters for what mainstream constitutional jurisprudence should be. Judges who embark on adventures outside those perimeters engage in judicial activism guided only by their own sense of ideology rather than the constitutional text.

Given this definition, the Court's decision in Varnum v. Brien (2009) can be described as nothing short of judicial activism. The "right" found by the Iowa Supreme Court is not, contrary to public opinion, the right to marry. The Court did in fact find a "right to sexual orientation," a nebulous concept the Court never bothered to define or limit in any way in its sixty-nine page opinion.

But the Court did more than declare a constitutional right to sexual orientation that must be entitled to all the marriage benefits that heterosexual couples enjoy. Rather, the Court determined that everyone has a right to self-identity. For in finding the right to sexual orientation, it determined that it is not necessary for sexual orientation to be an immutable characteristic.

As the Court rightly pointed out, a human trait that defines a group is "immutable" when the trait exists "solely by the accident of birth" or when the person with the trait has no ability to change it. The concept of immutability is important when examining an equal protection claim, because the "inability of a person to change a characteristic that is used to justify different treatment makes the discrimination violative of the rather basic concept of our system that legal burdens should bear some relationship to individual responsibility."

Knowing that science has not shown sexual orientation to be immutable, the Court redefined immutability to mean that "the identifying trait is so central to a person's identity that it would be abhorrent for government to penalize a person for refusing to change it." "Because sexual orientation is central to personal identity and may be altered, if at all, only at the expense of significant damage to the individual's sense of self," the Court held that sexual orientation is now a suspect class "entitled to [the same] consideration as...any other group that has been deemed to exhibit an immutable characteristic."

This concept of personal identity and sense of self is the new "right" found in the Iowa Constitution by a Court who embarked on judicial adventurism out of the originalism mainstream. Unfortunately, this right is neither new nor limited to sexual orientation or marriage but has also been used by courts to justify abortion and a right to die. It is the vogue (and vague) right used by courts when they want to read into the constitution rights that aren't there.

The elasticity of this new right can be found in the U.S. Supreme Court's rather utopian explanation of it in its decision in Planned Parenthood v. Casey (1992), n which it affirmed Roe v. Wade (1973):

> Our law affords constitutional protection to personal decisions relating to...matters[] involving the most intimate and personal choices a person may make in a lifetime, choices central to personal dignity and autonomy...
>
> At the heart of liberty is the right to define one's own concept of existence, of meaning, of the universe, and of the mystery of human life. Beliefs about these matters could not define the

> attributes of personhood were they formed under compulsion of the State. (emphasis added)

Given such an expansive individual right to self identity, government is only possible if its citizens unanimously and freely acquiesced their right to self identity when each new law is passed (a phenomenon not yet experienced in the history of mankind) or by its selective enforcement by the judiciary when it suits their purposes.

By picking and choosing which values constitute this right to self identity, our Supreme Court justices have taken upon themselves cart blanche authority to define for us what our identity really is. Judicial activism is an understatement for this coup d'etat by the Court.

Voting these justices out of office will not overturn Varnum, only a constitutional amendment will accomplish this in the long term. To that end, our efforts should be primarily focused on passing a constitutional amendment out of the statehouse or a constitutional convention. But at the same time, voters have every right, if not an obligation, to remove from office justices such as these who engage in judicial activism.

SELECTING JUDGES

(June 13, 2010)

In the final primary debate among Republican gubernatorial hopefuls, two of the candidates, both of which went on to lose the election, declared that they would impose a litmus test on judicial nominees. For that they were called naïve by the ultimately victorious GOP candidate because, under the current system, the governor has little choice over who he can nominate.

After one-hundred and five years of selecting judges by elections, Iowa adopted the so-called "Missouri Plan" or merit-based plan in 1962. Under this system, judicial vacancies are publicized and any qualified individual may apply.

These applicants are then "screened" by nominating committees who are made up of both attorneys and non-attorneys. The attorneys serving on the nominating commission are elected by their fellow attorneys, and the non-attorneys are appointed by the governor and confirmed by the Iowa Senate.

These committees are supposed to pick the two (or, in the case of appellate courts, three) most qualified candidates and forward their names to the governor, who then selects one of them to fill the vacancy. If the governor refuses to select one of the candidates, the selection then falls to the Chief Justice of the Iowa Supreme Court.

The current system does not allow a governor to tell the nominating commission to start the selection process over again when the individuals they forwarded to him fail his litmus test. When confronted with this after the final debate, Bob Vander Plaats, one of the two candidates who said he would only appoint judges who opposed homosexual marriage and abortion, stated that he would address this issue when it arose.

But the time to address this issue is now, before the issue ever arises. Rather than ducking this question, Vander Plaats should have responded that, in this age of judicial activism, the judicial selection process should be amended to reflect the need to ensure that judicial appointees would follow the law as it was originally understood rather than be guided by their own ideology.

Judicial activism is not confined to federal courts but has, in fact, found a home in many state courts. For instance, while six state supreme courts and one state trial court have held their states' bans on same-sex marriage to be unconstitutional, not one federal court has ever reached the same conclusion. The same ideologically-driven judicial philosophy has become widely accepted by a growing number of judges, regardless of whether they sit on the state or federal bench.

Judicial elections are hardly a solution to this problem because of their tendency to make those entrusted with the task of being impartial judges dependent upon big-money donors and ideological voting blocks. Rather, states such as Iowa who have the Missouri Plan should replace it in favor of the federal appointment process in which the president has complete discretion to choose his nominee who is then subject to confirmation by the Senate.

While this process would continue the Missouri Plan's tradition of avoiding the conflict of interest inherent in judicial elections, it would bring the Missouri Plan's "merit based" process out into the open. Instead of closed-door nominating commissions who are far too often dominated by the liberal state bar association, representatives directly responsible to the electorate would have the very public task of vetting nominees in open committee hearings.

In addition to merit, the president is free to nominate, and the senate free to confirm, those individuals who satisfy their judicial litmus test.

Some may object that, despite the federal nominating process, liberal judges have continued to find their way onto the bench. But that is not the fault of the system, but of senators who have too often failed to filibuster, or even threaten to filibuster, an activist nominee. At least, unlike the Missouri Plan, the federal selection process allows for a public debate over a particular nominee's judicial philosophy even if such a debate shamefully never occurs.

Obviously this change will not necessarily, in and of itself, cure judicial activism. However, rather than trying to solve the problem of judicial activism after it occurs, it is easier to solve it beforehand by weeding out potential judicial nominees with activist tendencies. This is something that the Missouri Plan —a closed door, unaccountable process too often dominated by fellow ideological activists—can never accomplish.

This change can only come about by a constitutional amendment, and Iowans should push for this amendment, in addition to a marriage amendment, to pass out of either the statehouse or a constitutional convention.

THE NEED FOR A STAY OF COURT DECISIONS
(June 21, 2010)

Though Bob Vander Plaats' proposed executive order "staying" the Iowa Supreme Court's decision last year legalizing same-sex marriage is misplaced, the idea of a temporary stay to allow the people to amend the Constitution has merit. Vander Plaats repeatedly said throughout the primary that the Court's decision put the "onus" back on the legislature, and he is right that they should have had the opportunity to act before the Court's decision went into effect.

The current Iowa Constitution, as is the case at the federal level and in all other states, does not provide a mechanism that would allow the legislature or the executive to delay a court decision. Once a court rules that a law or policy is unconstitutional, there is nothing to "stay" it from going into effect.

Courts may, on their own accord, postpone their decision to allow time for various motions to be filed. This is what the Supreme Court did in the same-sex marriage case when, following its procedural rules, it stayed the decision several weeks. Also, lower courts may delay their ruling while one party appeals the case to a higher court, which the trial court did in this case as well.

But there is no provision in the Constitution which provides for a court decision to be stayed, even if the Constitution is in the process of being amended to explicitly overturn the court's decision. Though a lower court's decision may be stayed pending an appeal to a higher court, there currently is no stay available when all appeals are exhausted save for the ultimate appeal to the people themselves.

Certainly such a temporary stay is warranted to see if We the People will take up that appeal and reverse the court's ruling. To use another analogy, both federal and state constitutions allow the legislature an opportunity to override an executive veto before it becomes final, yet there is no mechanism by which We the People can override a judicial veto before it takes effect.

Under the current system, the earliest (barring a constitutional convention) a constitutional marriage amendment could have been passed after the Iowa Supreme Court legalized same-sex marriage is 2012, three years and thousands of same-sex marriage licenses later. Once something becomes the law, whether a court ruling or a legislative bill, it becomes nearly impossible to repeal it.

Therefore, the Constitution should be amended to automatically stay for a period of forty-five days any court decision that finds a law or policy unconstitutional. The legislature does not have to do anything during those forty-five days, but if it does initially pass a constitutional amendment (the first of two votes needed by the legislature) in that time span, then the stay will be extended to allow for the General Assembly to vote on it a second time. Then, if it passes that hurdle, the stay will be continued until the amendment can come before the voters.

Under the Iowa Constitution, an amendment is ratified if a majority in both the Iowa House and Senate pass the proposed amendment in two consecutive terms of the General Assembly and a majority of the people subsequently approves the amendment at the next election.

Under this proposal, therefore, the Court's April 3, 2009, same-sex ruling would have been automatically stayed for forty-five days. If the Iowa legislature had initially passed a constitutional amendment within that time period, the stay would then be extended until the next consecutive term of the General Assembly (the 2011 or 2012 sessions) in order to allow the legislature an opportunity to pass it the second time around. If the legislature passes it a second time, the stay is further continued until the voters have a chance to vote on the amendment at the ballot box.

Unfortunately, this case has shown that at times the legislature will not pass a constitutional amendment, even if the overwhelming majority of the people want them to. Because of that, We the People must have the ability to place constitutional amendments directly on the ballot irrespective of political bosses in the statehouse. Even if, in general, one considers ballot initiatives a bad idea, they should at a minimum be allowed under this proposal for the limited purpose of checking the judiciary.

If the people had the right to place constitutional amendments directly on the ballot, under this proposal they would be given forty-five days after the court's ruling to gather enough signatures to place the amendment before the voters. If they were able to obtain the necessary number of signatures, then the stay would be extended until the voters had the opportunity to ratify the proposed amendment at the ballot box.

Amending the Constitution to allow for an automatic, temporary stay of court rulings does not make it easier for ill-advised amendments to be rushed through, to the later regret of voters. The amendment process itself will be unchanged (except for the possible inclusion of ballot initiatives), thereby continuing to ensure a thoughtful, deliberative waiting period during which proposed amendments can be thoroughly debated.

The only thing that will be changed is that the people will have a chance to engage in the process before judicial activism becomes law. It is important that the proposed stay be temporary and relatively short in order to ensure that our constitutional rule of law continues and that truly unconstitutional behavior is prevented.

However, it is equally important that We the People have a chance to overturn an unconstitutional law before it takes effect. This proposal aims to balance both of those vital interests by providing a brief automatic stay to allow the people the opportunity to begin the amendment process and, if they do, it temporarily extends the stay until the process runs its course.

The amendment process, and by consequence the temporary stay, cannot be extended forever. Under the current amendment process via the legislature, a proposed amendment must be passed in two consecutive terms of the General Assembly. It cannot be passed by the current General Assembly and then by another one in, for instance, 2020. The same rule should apply to amendments proposed via ballot initiatives.

It should be noted that if an amendment fails to pass under this proposal, it does not mean that the amendment can never pass at a later time. It simply means that if a proposed amendment fails along the line to ratification under this proposal, the temporary stay lapses and the court's decision takes effect. The same proposed amendment can still be ratified at a later time if the people so choose.

This proposal continues to allow the judiciary to serve as a check on unconstitutional laws and policies made by our elected officials, but it also allows We the People to serve as a check on the judiciary when it engages in judicial activism. In the end, Bob Vander Plaats was right that we need a stay on the judiciary, he was just wrong on how to implement it.

JUDICIAL TERM LIMITS

(June 20, 2010)

Effectively combating judicial adventurism outside the original mainstream requires creating institutional changes to the judiciary while maintaining its independence. Though we must work to pass a constitutional marriage amendment that will overturn the Iowa Supreme Court's ruling in Varnum v. Brien which legalized gay marriage, such an amendment, in and of itself, will not prevent future judicial activism.

Consequently, we also need to focus on constitutional amendments, either in the statehouse or at a constitutional convention, that will aid in combating judicial activism. While We the People have the right and duty to hold accountable the entire Supreme Court which held DOMA to be unconstitutional, voting them out of office will not, directly at least, overturn their decision.

Because only a constitutional amendment can reverse a court decision, the Constitution should be amended so as to allow for an automatic stay if the amendment process is started within forty-five days of the ruling. In addition, We the People must have the ability to effectively exercise the right of amendment through the use of ballot initiatives rather than relying on unresponsive party leaders in the statehouse.

In addition to amending the amendment process itself, the constitutional process of picking judges should be amended. By allowing the governor the ability to select judicial nominees and the senate the duty to confirm them, Iowans can allow for a debate over whether a particular nominee would follow the law as it was originally understood rather than be guided by his or her own ideology.

Not only should the selection process be changed, however, but the process of keeping judges should be changed in two significant ways—the frequency of retention votes should be increased, and judicial term limits should be established. Out of seven justices on the Iowa Supreme Court, only three stand for a retention vote this November—Chief Justice Marsha Ternus and Justices Michael Streit and David Baker.

Justice David Wiggins will not be up for retention until 2012, and Justices Mark Cady, David Hecht, and Brent Appel will not be on the ballot until 2016. The inability of the people to hold justices accountable for their unconstitutional decisions until years after they are made is unacceptable.

Currently, Supreme Court justices stand for retention votes every eight years, while appellate and trial court justices are on the ballot every six years. Such lengthy terms not only allow judicial activists to continue in office for years before they come before the voters, but they make it quite plausible that, by the time their name is placed on the ballot, their ideological adventurism will be forgotten by the voters.

In order to better hold judges accountable to the fundamental will of We the People as expressed in the Constitution, judges should stand for retention votes every two years. By creating a system whereby judges know they will have to stand before the voters in the very next election cycle, judges will be less tempted to engage in judicial activism. Though voting judges out of office should be reserved only for those cases in which judges venture outside the originalism mainstream, it should be a more immediate consequence rather than one years in the making.

Along with increasing the frequency of retention votes, judicial term limits should be established. Though, ideally, judges who engage in ideological jurisprudence unmoored from the Constitution should be removed from office by voters, the reality leaves much to be desired.

Since Iowa adopted the current system in 1962, only four judges have been removed from office, and none of them were removed for judicial activism. In fact, in 2004, voters refused to hold Woodbury County District Court Judge Jeffrey Neary accountable when he recognized an out-of-state same-sex marriage as lawfully binding in this state in order to subsequently divorce the couple.

Because retention votes have yet to hold any judge accountable who ventures outside of the originalism mainstream, term of ten years should be established as a failsafe to ensure that such judges do not necessarily continue in office until the mandatory retirement age of 72.

Currently, Iowa has five appellate judges who have served longer than a decade, and two more who will reach that milestone next year. Automatic removal from the proverbial judicial monastery to the ranks of practicing attorneys and ordinary citizens will also have the added benefit of keeping judges from becoming too enticed with their own power.

By themselves, few of these proposals will serve as much of a check on judicial activism. Together, however, constitutional amendments that would provide for temporary stays and ballot initiatives in the amendment process itself, change the way judges are nominated, increase the frequency of retention votes, and provide for judicial term limits will provide We the People with adequate tools for taming the least dangerous branch.

IF IT IS NOT DECLARATIONAL, THEN IT IS NOT CONSTITUTIONAL?

(July 4, 2010)

On this day 234 years ago, our Founders declared that "these United Colonies are, and of a Right ought to be Free and Independent States [and] that they are Absolved from all Allegiance to the British Crown." Increasingly, our country's birth certificate is being cited among conservative activists as binding legal authority to check the liberal agenda of both legislatures and the courts.

As one proponent has put it, "[o]ur American Declaration is the supreme, unamendable moral law of the United States. Declarational law preceded and trumps our supreme, amendable secular law, the Constitution. As stated in our Declaration, the purpose of secular law (Constitution) is to secure our sacred, unalienable, equal, individual rights to life, liberty, and pursuit of happiness."

Because of this, it has been argued that "if a law passed by Congress, or an executive order issued by the President, or a court opinion issued by Judges runs contrary to the principles of the Declaration, then it runs contrary to the spirit of the Constitution. In other words, if it is not Declarational, then it is not Constitutional."

Such "undeclarational" laws may not necessarily violate the express provisions of the Constitution itself. Rather, advocates of this theory argue that, even if Congress, the President, or the judiciary do have the Constitutional authority to do something, a particular use of that power may run afoul the "spirit" of the Declaration and, consequently the Constitution itself.

The sole purpose, therefore, of "Declarational" law is to allow for its advocates to read into the Constitution ideas and prohibitions which are no where in the text of the document itself but which proponents of the theory sincerely believe to be mandated by the "spirit" of the Declaration.

Many are unabashed in their attempts to find every conservative principle mandated by the Declaration, and thus by the Constitution, arguing that the former "contains all the principles of the Conservative Movement: belief in God, Divine purpose, Natural Law, Natural Rights, the sweep of history, the definition of tyranny, unalienable rights, the purpose of government, private property, free enterprise, civil justice, the just war theory, and everything in the Bill of Rights."

Taking up this theme, Christian law professor Herbert Titus stated on Jan Mickelson's morning talk show on WHO Radio on April 14, 2009, that both our state and federal governments are bound by the Creator-centric worldview of the Declaration's natural law. He went so far as to say that, though both the state and federal constitutions are completely silent on the subject, the Levitical definition of marriage became constitutionally binding, via the Declaration, on both the legislature and the judiciary, who are powerless to change it.

Because the Iowa Supreme Court "attempt[ed] to make straight what God has made crooked" when they legalized same-sex marriage, Titus argued that their decision was wrong because "[t]hey are usurping the authority of God" in violation of their duty under the Declaration of Independence.

That is not a legal argument but rather a moral one which, however much one may prefer the biblical definition of marriage, has no place in constitutional argument. In our secular constitutional republic, the Bible does not determine whether something is constitutional. While "Declarational" law or natural law binds the conscience and can serve as the impetus for new legislation or the civil disobedience of existing law, the Founders simply did not establish it as the supreme law of the land.

It would be odd, indeed, if they had intended to graft the Declaration's references to "the Laws of Nature and Nature's God" into the Constitution without saying so. The men who labored under the summer heat of 1787 to create a document of limited, enumerated powers never once contemplated making "Declarational" law on par with the Constitution as the "supreme law of the land."

Even if they had wanted to enshrine "Declarational" law into the Constitution, that document would have been an odd place to do so because the federal government had no power to either violate "Declarational" law or to enforce it. It has very little power to enact domestic legislation (which is why the Founders did not originally include a Bill of Rights), and provisions for Congress to enforce constitutional protections against the states were not added until later amendments.

Additionally, the idea that the Founders intended to include "Declarational" law along with the Constitution as the supreme law of the land is contradicted by the fact that they codified in the later a violation of that law. Without mentioning it by the name of slavery, the Constitution not only included bondsmen in determining population for the apportionment of House seats, but it also forbade

Congress from prohibiting the foreign importation of slaves until 1808. Few, if any, Founders justified slavery as moral, yet they included that violation of "Declarational" law into the Constitution itself.

In short, "Declarational" law is an enticing, but an ultimately perilous, temptation because it allows conservatives to read into the Constitution what they want it to say, even if the Constitution is silent on those subjects. As a theory of constitutional interpretation it simply becomes the conservative version of the liberal's "living Constitution"—the means of interpreting the Constitution to achieve one's ideological goals.

The Constitution does not mandate every conservative principle, and the constitutionalist rejects the offer, no matter how tempting, to do so through Declarationalism. We do not need biblical judges, capitalist judges, Lockean judges, Burkean judges, Aquinasian judges, or any other strand of conservatism that can be found in the Declaration.

Rather, we only need constitutionalist judges who will interpret that document as its text was originally understood, leaving morality and conservatism to be fought for in the political and cultural arenas. Those who advocate for "Declarationalist" activist judges (while at the same time claiming that courts have no power) should be wary of courts judging morality, for they may not get the type of "righteous" judges they hope for.

KAGAN FAILED HER OWN TEST

(July 15, 2010)

In a 1995 law review article entitled Confirmation Messes, Old and New, Supreme Court nominee Elena Kagan wrote: "The problem [with judicial confirmation hearings] is not that the Senate focused too much on a nominee's legal views, but that it did so far too little....The kind of inquiry that would contribute most to understanding and evaluating a nomination is ... [a] discussion first, of the nominee's broad judicial philosophy and, second, of her views on particular constitutional issues...."

Without such a forthright and honest discussion of a nominee's judicial philosophy, Kagan worried that contemporary confirmation hearings were becoming nothing more than a "vapid and hollow charade." In an interview by the Metropolitan Corporate Council published in May 2004, Kagan reiterated the need for authentic Senate confirmation hearings because "[t]he attitude and views that a person brings to the bench make a difference in how they reached those decisions, so the Senate is right to take an interest in who these people are and what they believe."

Unfortunately, Kagan's performance during her hearings did little to shed light on the specific attitudes and views she would bring to the bench. We did learn that, though she famously stated at her hearings that "we are all originalists now," Kagan showed signs that her fidelity to the Constitution's original understanding only goes so far. For instance, Kagan stated that "there are a range of other kinds of provisions in the Constitution of a much more general kind. And -- and those provisions were meant to be interpreted over time, to be applied to new situations and new factual contexts."

And how is a judge supposed to interpret these general provisions in the Constitution? While claiming not to know what a progressive jurist is, Kagan gave a very progressive answer to that question when she said that such provisions should be interpreted by the promise of liberty contained in the Constitution's preamble. Though courts have long held the preamble to be simply rhetorical rather than a grant of power, Kagan praised this changing (i.e., progressive) ideal of liberty as her default "original understanding" of the Constitution.

Kagan further disproved that she is actually an originalist when she discussed with senators the process by which the Constitution is changed. While stating that the formal amendment process is important, Kagan proceeded to state that courts can also bring change to the Constitution by disregarding its original understanding. She specifically cited Brown v. Board of Education as an example of doing what you think is right "and eventually the law will catch up" (ignoring the fact, as all liberals do, that Brown can be defended on originalist grounds).

As Kagan put it in response to a question by Senator Kohl, "I think that there are some circumstances in which looking to the original intent is the determinative thing in a case and other circumstances in which it is likely not to be." Unfortunately, she refused to address under which circumstances she may be a progressive jurist rather than an originalist. When asked if she agreed with past precedent, even those she may have decided differently if she had been on the Court when they were made, she constantly intoned that such cases are "settled law going forward," though she was careful to maintain that they are only "entitled to all the weight that precedent usually gets" and that "there are various reasons for why you might overturn a precedent."

Rather than settling for mere lip service towards past precedent, senators should have, as Kagan herself wrote in her 1995 law review article, insisted "on seeing how theory works in practice by evoking a nominee's comments on particular issues —involving privacy rights, free speech, race and gender discrimination, and so forth—that the Court regularly faces."

Confirmation hearings are a job interview, and senators must demand that a job applicant explain his or her legal philosophy by using specific examples from past precedent. While discussing hypothetical questions regarding future laws and facts may cause a nominee to prejudge a case that may later appear before his court, there is no such danger in discussing past cases. Just as a judge does not have to recuse himself in a pending First Amendment case because he dealt with First Amendment precedent in a similar case last month, so too a nominee would not have to recuse himself for simply discussing precedent during his confirmation hearings.

Kagan, in her 1995 law review article, set the proper standard for confirmation hearings for all job applicants for the federal bench, a standard which she obstinately refused to satisfy. Consequently, as Senator Specter wrote in his 2000 autobiography Passion for Truth: "In my judgment, the Senate should resist, if not refuse to confirm, Supreme Court nominees who refuse to answer questions on fundamental issues."

IS COURT-STRIPPING THE SOLUTION?

(August 16, 2010)

Some commentators in Iowa have argued that adding a marriage amendment to the Iowa constitution is unnecessary. Rather, they maintain that the legislature has the authority to remove from the courts any jurisdiction to review the constitutionality of a statute. As a result, proponents believe that there is no need to amend the Iowa Constitution when the legislature can simply thank the Supreme Court for their opinion, but continue to enforce the current law without recourse to judicial review.

Though the idea of court-stripping has only recently begun to gain traction in Iowa, it is an old idea that was first used in 1801 when the newly-elected Jeffersonian Congress, rightly afraid that the Supreme Court would hold their abolishment of federal judgeships unconstitutional, removed the Court's jurisdiction to review their actions. At the time, the courts never ruled on the constitutionality of court-stripping because it was never litigated.

As support for their argument, proponents of court-stripping cite Article III, Section 2, Clause 2 of the U.S. Constitution, which provides that the Supreme Court shall have "appellate Jurisdiction, both as to Law and Fact, with such Exceptions, and under such Regulations as the Congress shall make." Iowa's Constitution contains somewhat similar language in Sections 4 and 6 of Article 5.

At the federal level, court-stripping has become a favorite "magic wand" by conservatives in their effort to check activist judges who do not adhere to the Constitution as it was originally understood. Each year, court-stripping bills are unsuccessfully introduced in Congress to remove the jurisdiction of federal courts to hear challenges to the federal Defense of Marriage Act, the Pledge of Allegiance, abortion regulations, etc.

But as much as we may desire such an easy solution, the Exemptions Clause (the court-stripping provision) was never intended by the Founders as a tool by which Congress could combat judicial tyranny. There is not a single Founder at the time the Constitution was drafted and ratified who proposed any other check to reign in the judiciary than impeachment and the amendment process. Never once did they suggest any recourse to the Exemptions Clause, an executive order vetoing court decisions, or nullification.

Rather, the Exemption Clause only gave Congress the authority to regulate the appellate jurisdiction of one court—the Supreme Court. By its own terms, the Clause only refers to the "supreme Court" and therefore does not give Congress the authority to regulate the jurisdiction of lower federal courts or state courts. Nor do state legislatures have the authority to strip federal courts of jurisdiction to hear challenges to their state laws.

Additionally, early drafts of the Clause at the Constitutional Convention illustrate that it was only intended to provide Congress with the power to distribute appellate review between the Supreme Court and such lower federal courts that Congress may establish. These preliminary versions stated that the Supreme Court shall have such appellate review "with such exceptions and under such regulations as the Legislature shall make. The Legislature may assign any part of the jurisdiction above mentioned (except the trial of the President of the United States) in the manner, and under the limitations which it shall think proper, to such Inferior Courts, as it shall constitute from time to time." (emphasis original)

Alexander Hamilton, writing in Federalist No. 81, explained that the degree of the Supreme Court's review of lower court decisions will necessarily vary as to the type of case (criminal, civil, admiralty, etc.). Because of this, it was impossible to draft a single standard into the Constitution and, therefore, the Constitutional Convention opted to leave it to "the national legislature [to] prescribe [such regulations so as to] enable the government to modify it in such a manner as will best answer the ends of public justice and security."

Apart from a historical analysis, the Exemptions Clause cannot be read to allow Congress to exempt itself from judicial review, for doing so would make it a law unto itself. While conservatives desire such a power for use against activist judges, liberals would be all too eager to use it to insulate their legislative agendas from constitutional scrutiny.

Though conservatives relish the idea of stripping the courts of their authority to strike down abortion regulations, the defense of marriage act (DOMA), and the Pledge of Allegiance, they are naturally outraged when the Democrats contemplate doing the same with ObamaCare, cap and trade, bailout programs, oil drilling moratoriums, the Fairness Doctrine, Card Check, etc.

Treating the Exemption Clause in this manner would give Congress a "get out of jail free" card whereby it could commit constitutional violations without fear of being caught. Furthermore, there would be no need for an amendment process to the Constitution, nor even a written Constitution itself, because change could occur by simple legislative fiat insulated from judicial review.

For instance, though the current judicial nomination process is established by the state constitution, if court stripping were permissible the General Assembly could simply change the process by statute and remove from the courts any power to review their actions. Certainly the Exemptions Clause was never understood to provide the legislature with this type of an end run around the Constitution.

But in Iowa there is also a very real practical problem with this magic wand, for even if the General Assembly stripped the courts of their authority to review the constitutionality of DOMA, it will still be up to each individual county recorder, the officer charged with issuing marriage licenses, as to whether they will follow the Iowa Supreme Court's ruling in Varnum v. Brien or the state's stricken, but now non-reviewable, DOMA.

Because the legislature and governor have no authority to force them to obey DOMA, it will be up to the Iowa Attorney General to determine whether or not, in his or her opinion, the county recorders are following the law and, if they are not, to institute removal procedures against them. Those procedures, however, bring the issue back before the courts, the very judges the legislature was trying to avoid in the first place.

A constitutionally dubious proposition such as court-stripping is not the solution to restoring traditional marriage in Iowa, only a constitutional amendment is.

AN IMPROVEMENT WE DESPERATELY NEED
(September 9, 2010)

Credit to the Des Moines Register for actually discussing what the Iowa State Bar Association and Iowans for Fair and Impartial Courts have so far avoided—amending the Iowa Constitution to model the judicial selection process after the federal system. These groups would like voters to think that there are only two possible ways of selecting judges

—Iowa's current use of the Missouri Plan or judicial elections.

But the Register actually had the gumption to mention the third choice, an option advocated by Republican gubernatorial candidate Terry Branstad and others. In the end, however, the Register was less than impressed with the idea, writing in a recent editorial that such a change would bring the "circus" of federal nomination hearings to the Iowa Capital.

"Far from being an improvement," the Register opined, "this would assure perennial political battles over selecting judges. It almost certainly would politicize Iowa's process: The governor would feel compelled to play to his or her political base by nominating judges who fit a particular ideological mold; the members of the General Assembly (presumably the Senate) not of the governor's party would feel obligated to find dirt on nominees; and the nominees themselves would be pigeonholed based on their party affiliations."

In a recent article in The Iowa Independent, Mark Kende, the James Madison Chair in constitutional law at Drake Law School, agreed, arguing that "what would be lost is the fact that you then have a process that is more politicized. Inevitably then, when you elect governors, you're not just electing governors, but you're in a sense coming close to starting to elect the judiciary."

While the federal judicial nominating process may bring partisan and ideological differences into the open, the Register is disingenuous in claiming that Iowa's current system is not already politicized. The overwhelming number of judges and nominating commission members are Democrats, and this result is repeated in other states who have adopted the Missouri Plan. The Register has not only refused to discuss this issue, but recently rejected a guest op-ed detailing these statistics.

The Register is right to point out that the federal confirmation hearings have become a "circus." Federal judicial nominees, especially for the Supreme Court, are subject to strict scrutiny and can face grueling confirmation battles. Senators, with increasing frequency, are preventing nominees from making it out of committee or, when they do, threatening to filibuster a full-Senate vote. And the lucky ones who actually are confirmed have to wait months, if not years, before they can assume their seat on the federal bench.

This is a circus, however, that we need to have. The process is not so much a circus in which politicians hope to score points, but rather a conflict over the ideological makeup of the federal courts which have far-ranging consequences for the future of our country. As a result of the political seduction of the law, whoever controls the judiciary controls which policies and "minority rights" will be favored.

As has been previously noted, this is a power struggle over the meaning of the Constitution—either judges are bound by the text and original public understanding of the document, or they are free to be guided by their empathy and sense of justice as they engage in "goal oriented" jurisprudence.

Democrats have long understood that what is at stake is not just abstract ideology but political power—the ability to win in the courts what they can't at the ballot box. The statistics show that it is foolish to assume that Democrats will not seek to control the judiciary simply because judges are nominated by "merit-based" commissions. Sadly, the opposite has occurred as Democrats have been able to gain control of the process without public scrutiny and accountability.

Some conservatives, favoring judicial elections, argue that the federal nominating process doesn't prevent liberals from assuming the bench, even when a Republican president is in office. For instance, Justices O'Connor, Kennedy, and Souter were all nominated by Republican presidents but fell far short of conservative expectations.

But those results were not the fault of the process, but of the process not being used. For far too long Republican politicians did not fully understand what was at stake, or seek to use the process with the same vigor and dedication of the Left. But presidents and senators alike must apply a constitutional litmus test by seeking a nominee's views of past precedent to judge his or her adherence to originalism.

Furthermore, the process can be amended to provide additional checks on judicial activism by providing for more frequent retention votes, term limits, and a temporary stay of court decisions. The federal model, with these modifications, provide the transparency and accountability to the process that the current system desperately lacks, while avoiding the money and special interests too often inherent in judicial elections.

This is the debate we should be having, but obviously the liberals in the Democratic Party, Bar Association, and media have no interest in an honest and open debate that might lead to changes that would erode their influence over a judiciary they currently control behind closed doors.

OUR ENLIGHTENED MASTERS

(October 18, 2010)

Recently the Des Moines Register penned an editorial in which, in essence, they told Iowans that they should bend over and take it like a man rather than vote any justice off the Iowa Supreme Court. The constant theme throughout the editorial was that Iowans should not retaliate against judges who are simply interpreting an evolving Constitution.

The Register praised the Court's decision in Varnum v. Brien (2009) to legalize same-sex marriage because it "is consistent with the Iowa Supreme Court's long record of recognizing equal rights of minority groups." The Register went on to argue that Varnum "is the only reasonable reading of the plain language of the Iowa Bill of Rights, which says, 'All men and women are, by nature, free and equal' and that 'the general assembly shall not grant to any citizen, or class of citizens, privileges or immunities, which, upon the same terms shall not equally belong to all citizens.'"

The Register failed to present any evidence that those who drafted and ratified those constitutional provisions in 1857 understood them to require the state to recognize homosexual marriage.

To the contrary, the Register asserted that "equal rights guaranteed by the constitution cannot be restricted by contemporary social convention."

In other words, they view that Constitution as a living, evolving document that is not bound by its original public understanding but must be interpreted anew by the Supreme Court. Going a step further, the Register praised the Iowa Supreme Court for its history of often being "decades ahead of the U.S. Supreme Court" and the "norms of their time" in recognizing new constitutional rights.

Their view of the role of a judge, therefore, is not simply to reinterpret the Constitution in order to bring it up to current societal standards, but to actually lead the way by going beyond "contemporary social convention" to protect yet undiscovered minority groups. The progressive, elitist judge is threatened, according to the Register, by retention votes that would "transform the judicial process into a popular political forum."

The Court itself in Varnum embraced this progressive role of judging, writing that a statute must be declared unconstitutional "even though it may be supported by strong and deep-seated traditional beliefs and popular opinion." The Court continued that "citizens' rights are [not] constrained to those previously recognized."

Elaborating on its self-assigned role as social shepherds, the Court argued, "Our responsibility, however, is to protect constitutional rights of individuals from legislative enactments that have denied those rights, even when the rights have not yet been broadly accepted, were at one time unimagined, or challenged a deeply ingrained practice of law viewed to be impervious to the passage of time."

Quoting the U.S. Supreme Court decision in Lawrence v. Texas (2003) which found a federal constitutional right to sodomy, the Iowa Supreme Court wrote that "'times can blind us to certain truths and later generations can see that laws once thought necessary and proper in fact serve only to oppress' and as our constitution 'endures, persons in every generation can invoke its principles in their own search for greater freedom' and equality."

In turning to the definition of equal protection, the Court argued that "equal protection can only be defined by the standards of each generation." Quoting liberal law professor Cass Sunstein, they wrote that the "'Equal Protection Clause looks forward, serving to invalidate practices that were widespread at the time of its ratification and that were expected to endure.'"

Continuing, they maintain that a "classification persists until a new understanding of equal protection is achieved. The point in time when the standard of equal protection finally takes a new form is a product of the conviction of one, or many, individuals that a particular grouping results in inequality and the ability of the judicial system to perform its constitutional role free from the influences that tend to make society's understanding of equal protection resistant to change."

The justices of the Iowa Supreme Court no longer feel bound to interpret the Constitution as it was originally publicly understood. Rather, they see it as their job to impose their own political, moral, and social ideals on Iowans as they lead us toward a higher plane of enlightenment. They believe it is their responsibility to guide us past our fear, guns, and religion to the better angels of our nature.

And they, like the Register, are shocked and dismayed that the public isn't taking it like a man when they embark on this type of adventurism outside the originalism mainstream. The campaign to oust the judges is not only a threat to their job security, but to their entire worldview of societal improvement via judicial fiat.

This isn't a fight over judicial independence or the influx of money in judicial elections. Rather, this is a fight over the proper role of judges in interpreting the fundamental will of the people as expressed in a written Constitution. It is time for the people of Iowa to refuse to bend over but rather stand up and tell the judges that they will lose their jobs if they stray from the Constitution. This is certainly an intimidation campaign, but an entirely justified and proper one.

But while it is our right and responsibility to remove judges who pretend to be our enlightened master, Iowans must remember that the retention vote is only the first battle in the war against judicial activism. Real and permanent change can only come about when the judicial branch is changed through amending the state constitution.

THE MEANING OF THE WORD "IS"

(October 20, 2010)

Bill Clinton infamously responded to a question during his deposition by saying that, "It depends on what the meaning of the word 'is' is." Words have different meanings depending on context, and the role of the judge is to determine the meaning of the language used in a statute, regulation, prior court decision, or constitutional provision and apply that meaning to a particular case.

This job is particularly important when a judge is determining the meaning of the Constitution because it is the embodiment of the fundamental will of the people. If we apply our own meaning to that document, rather than that of those who drafted and ratified it, then we have changed what they said. But the Constitution is the supreme law of the land, and neither its text nor its meaning can be changed by any other means than the laborious amendment process.

It is imperative, therefore, that the Constitution be read by judges according to the original public understanding of its words and phrases. To apply any other meaning would be to substitute the judges' will in place of the supreme and fundamental will of the people who ratified that document.

This simple, common sense approach is used by courts in interpreting legislative statutes, wills, divorce decrees, or administrative regulations. For instance, there has yet to be a lower court who, in applying a decision of a higher court, has disregarded what that higher court meant in favor of a new, evolving standard.

Yet, when it comes to the Constitution, courts routinely claim the power to interpret it according to evolving societal standards. The reason for this is simple—due to the unwillingness of the majority of the people to act legislatively, the judges' desired result will only become a reality when the courts act as social shepherds.

This is precisely what the Iowa Supreme Court did in Varnum v. Brien (2009) when it legalized same-sex marriage. Far from simply "doing their job," they were substituting their own will in place of that of those who ratified our state constitution. Never once did the Court attempt to produce any evidence that those who gave us our current Constitution in 1857 understood its equal protection guaranty to mandate same-sex marriage.

Some have argued that the Constitution was written in broad language precisely so it could be reinterpreted with each generation. But the language of the Constitution is broad for the simple reason that it is a constitution; it was never intended to, in the words of Chief Justice John Marshall in Marbury v. Madison (1803), have the "prolixity of a legal code."

Additionally, there is no evidence in the historical record that the Founding Generation ever intended to assign such a sweeping, authoritarian power to the judicial branch. To the contrary, those who drafted and ratified the Constitution assigned it such a limited role in our system of government that in Federalist 78 Alexander Hamilton called it the least dangerous branch.

The very idea of establishing a majority of attorneys sitting on the highest court as a naked power organ would have been repulsive to a generation who had committed their lives, fortunes, and sacred honor to a war of liberty against an unaccountable, centralized government. They feared giving government too much power and strived to create a democratically-elected government of internal checks and balances that exercised limited, enumerated powers.

Proponents of such a judicial oligarchy also fail to explain how, if the Constitution is in fact evolving, such changing mores may not also result in certain rights, even those explicitly guaranteed in the Constitution, from being limited. Though the very purpose of the Constitution is to protect certain rights from government interference, an evolving

Constitution would make all rights dependent on the will of current societal values.

But, assuming for the moment that the courts were intended to interpret an evolving Constitution with each new generation, proponents of such judicial activism provide us little guidance on how they are supposed to accomplish such a mission. In fact, these proponents decry the use of every available means by which judges could measure an evolving society.

For instance, they claim judges cannot be elected because they might be susceptible to the whims of the majority of the people. They argue vigorously against the use of public opinion polls, and shudder at the very notion of putting such issues to a vote of the people.

They ridicule the federal model whereby those directly responsible to the people can inquire into a judicial nominee's sense of society's evolution. And they even go so far as to claim that a majority of the people cannot vote judges off the bench if they happen to erroneously guess current societal mores; a guess, by the way, that they needed to arrive at by only a simple majority.

Without these methods, it is impossible for judges to measure how far a society's values may have evolved. But that is precisely the point. Rather than allowing democracy to run its course as a changing society enacts legislation reflecting its evolution, judges see it as their role to lead such a society to where all but a small, judicially-favored minority want it to go.

This isn't judging, but activism; this isn't interpreting the Constitution, but dictating from the bench. The effort to remove the Iowa Supreme Court justices on November 2nd is not because they may have gotten a single decision wrong. Rather, it is because they have set themselves above the fundamental will of We the People as expressed in our written state constitution.

Sadly, however, this activism has become the norm among the liberal elite who make up our judiciary, bar association, and law schools. It is the reason why so many liberals, from billionaire George Soros to all three pro-retention groups here in Iowa, are defending the current system which they dominate from start to finish. And this is why the judicial branch needs to undergo a fundamental change via a constitutional amendment, either at a constitutional convention or through the legislative route.

This is a battle over who is supreme—the fundamental will of the people as expressed in their written Constitution, or the whims of a majority of a handful of cloistered attorneys. When voting this November, vote to remove the three state supreme court justices, to hold a constitutional convention to make needed changes to the system, and for state senators and representatives who will work to make the judicial branch the least dangerous branch once again.

MR. LIVING CONSTITUTION

(May 4, 2012)

In remarks at Drake Law School's inaugural Iowa Constitution Lecture Series in March, the Chief Justice of the Iowa Supreme Court made the remarkable assertion that he is Mr. Constitution, literally. Proclaiming that our "Iowa Constitution has always been a living constitution," Chief Justice Cady assigned to the Court the role of being the living embodiment of that Constitution.

In Cady's view, the seven justices of the Supreme Court are a continuous constitutional convention unto themselves, redefining terms and phrases as they "sort through the growing understanding to give greater meaning to equality over time..." They are a judicial cabal whose job it is to "sort through each controversy to draw out the true will of the people" that Iowa's founding generation, and even contemporary society, may be blind to.

Cady acknowledges that "originalism naturally flows from the way courts have functioned in interpreting law in general," such "as with statutes." However, he posits two theories as to why why this simple and routine approach does not apply to the Iowa Supreme Court in interpreting the state's constitution.

First, he argues, originalism "is simply inconsistent with the approach Iowa embraced a century and a half ago and has consistently followed throughout history. Originalism has not been Iowa's way." He is unable, however, to cite a single quote from anyone during the period that Iowa's Constitution was drafted and ratified who understood that document to create a judicial oligarchy.

Instead, he cites two 19th century cases in which the Court ended segregation in schools and public accommodations, praising his predecessors for "engag[ing] in analysis that considered the meaning of equality that was taking shape at the time in Iowa...Society at the time was changing its understanding of blacks, and so too did the constitutional principle of equality."

A tyrant does not became any less tyrannical simply because he laid claim to dictatorial powers long ago and may occasionally have reached just results. Ends do not justify the means, no matter how much we may applaud them. Though explicitly rejected by Cady, "changes to [the constitution] sought by later generations [is] to come [only] by the formal democratic process of amending the constitution, not by judicial decisions."

Secondly, Cady argues that originalism has no place in Iowa because the public "has never rejected a constitutional decision of the Iowa Supreme Court over the last 155 years through the constitutional process of amendment." Instead, '"even when a new principle of equality has been applied in a way that was greeted by the public with displeasure or surprise, Iowans have chosen the contemplative approach..."

Cady confuses the inability of voters to overcome the high hurdle of passing a constitutional amendment with public "acceptance of the court's [role] to carefully and accurately sort through each controversy to draw out the true will of the people." To state that a tyrant has yet to be checked is hardly the same as saying the citizens have accepted his power as legitimate. Just ask the three justices removed by voters in 2010 for their role in the 2009 Varnum decision.

In a revealing statement, Cady insists that this alleged public acceptance occurs because the "Iowa Supreme Court has never led the public down a path of individual rights that it refused to go." For Cady, the Court's job is to be our enlightened masters, imposing their own political, moral, and social ideals on Iowans as they lead us toward a higher plane of enlightenment. He believes it is their responsibility to guide us past our fear, guns, and religion to the better angels of our nature.

He praised Varnum for the Court's role in opening "the door to the public's increased understanding of marriage equality." In authoring that decision, Cady wrote that "equal protection can only be defined by the standards of each generation" and that it is the Court's role to lead a reluctant society to "a new understanding of equal protection."

Rather than allowing democracy to run its course as a changing society enacts legislation reflecting its evolution, Cady sees it as the Court's role to lead society to where none but a small, judicially-favored minority want it to go. This isn't judging, but activism; this isn't interpreting the Constitution, but dictating from the bench.

This is not "the constitutional way of life in Iowa," but an attempt by some of the justices to set themselves above the fundamental will of We the People as expressed in our written constitution. This is judicial tyranny.

2 FEDERALISM

THE FOLLY OF '98

(April 7, 2010)

In the aftermath of the passage of Obamacare, eighteen states have joined together to file suit in order to have the act declared an unconstitutional power grab by the federal government. There are some commentators, however, who have urged a different approach to this and other unconstitutional acts of Congress—the Principles of '98.

By this they refer to the Kentucky and Virginia Resolutions of 1798, written by Thomas Jefferson and James Madison respectively, which declared that individual states are free to declare unconstitutional acts of Congress "void, and of no force."

The second Kentucky Resolution, passed in 1979, reads

> That, if those who administer the general government be permitted to transgress the limits fixed by that compact, by a total disregard to the special delegations of power therein contained, an annihilation of the state governments, and the

creation, upon their ruins, of a general consolidated government, will be the inevitable consequence:

That the principle and construction, contended for by sundry of the state legislatures, that the general government is the exclusive judge of the extent of the powers delegated to it, stop nothing short of despotism —since the discretion of those who administer the government, and not the Constitution, would be the measure of their powers:

That the several states who formed that instrument, being sovereign and independent, have the unquestionable right to judge of its infraction; and, That a nullification, by those sovereignties, of all unauthorized acts done under color of that instrument, is the rightful remedy. (Emphasis original).

The Principles of '98, which were immediately condemned by ten other state legislatures, provided the foundation for the Hartford Convention, the Nullification Crises of 1832, and eventually session and the Civil War. The basis underlying this folly is the misconstruction of our form of government from one of We the People to a confederacy of states.

Building on this idea of a confederacy, the Folly of '98 holds that two co-equal sovereigns—the federal government and the states—can co-exist in the same union. But such coexistence is impossible —either the states must yield to the federal government or the federal government must yield to the states. If we are to exist as one nation, federal law must, as the Constitution puts it, be "the supreme law of the land."

But the Folly of '98 goes a step further and argues that, not only are the federal and state governments co-equal, but that each state is a co-equal sovereign to each other. Such a theory makes a mockery of this "confederacy" of the states because it gives the minority power over the majority. For if a significant minority of states threatened not to obey a law passed by Congress, it would do Congress little good to pass it, resulting in the transformation of our government from majoritarian representation of We the People to a system much like the United Nation's Security Council in which one member has a veto on all the others.

The natural outcome of such a stalemate among states who are equal sovereigns is armed conflict. The Folly of '98 makes secession and civil war not only a viable but a likely alternative for disputing states who are unable to find agreement on essential issues such as commercial regulations, a national bank, or the mobilization of national guard troops for war.

And armed conflict is all the more likely when there is no longer any national court system to arbitrate disputes. For if the states can nullify Congressional acts such as Obamacare, than certainly they can also nullify federal court rulings on issues such as national regulations, abortion, and Miranda warnings. But without resort to the courts, there is only resort to the sword.

No matter how disguised it is in constitutional shenanigans, the Folly of '98 has no room in our national debates, for in the end it leads to disunion, rebellion, and civil war.

IS LESS DEMOCRACY ACTUALLY MORE DEMOCRACY? (June 9, 2010)

Should this be the last year that the American people directly vote for their U.S. Senators? In the name of more democracy, several Republican nominees have recently expressed an openness to the idea of repealing the 17th Amendment, the 1913 amendment which replaced the original selection of senators by state legislatures with a direct vote of the people.

Ohio's Steve Strivers and Idaho's Raul Labrador, both Republican nominees for the House, have indicated that they are sympathetic with the idea. One of the Tea Party candidates who defeated Senator Robert Bennett (R-UT) last month, Tim Bridgewater, has argued that "if the states elected their senators, legislative monstrosities like ObamaCare or [No Child Left Behind], with their burdensome mandates, would never see the light of day."

That, precisely, was the reason why our country's Founders provided states with a voice in the federal government. Because they knew that constitutional limits on federal power were meaningless if the courts refused to enforce them, they also devised institutional checks and balances in the structure of the federal government so that, as James Madison wrote, each of the "constituent parts may...be the means of keeping each other in their proper places."

Politicians are, collectively, addicts to power, and history has shown that they know no self-control. Because, as Lord Acton aptly noted, "power tends to corrupt, and absolute power corrupts absolutely," the Framers of our Constitution feared giving too much power to the federal government and instead made it one of specific and limited powers.

Since politicians cannot be trusted to keep themselves within their constitutional bounds, the Founders made some of them directly accountable to the states, a constituency which had the ability and the will to resist any encroachment on their constitutional prerogatives. By this means, the ambition of the states would check the ambition of the federal government.

If the states ever lost their voice in the federal government, the Founders knew that they would eventually become mere handmaidens of unrestrained national power and that federalism, that great preserver of the greatest amount of liberty for the American people, would be dead.

James Madison wrote in The Federalist Papers that the election of Senators by state legislatures was necessary to "giv[e] the State governments such an agency in the formation of the federal government as [to] secure the authority of the former." Roger Sherman argued at the Constitutional Convention that, "[i]f the State [governments] are to be continued, it is necessary in order to preserve harmony between the Nation and State [governments] that the elections to the former [should] be made by the later."

George Mason stressed at the Convention that without adequate protection "the national Legislature [would] swallow up the legislatures of the States. The protection from this occurrence [would] be the securing to the state legislatures the choice of the senators of the United States."

Alexander Hamilton, strident nationalist though he was, noted in The Federalist Papers that, without the election of senators by state legislatures, "it would doubtless have been interpreted into an entire dereliction of the federal principle, and would certainly have deprived the State governments of that absolute safeguard which they will enjoy under this provision."

The fears of the Founders came to pass, however, when the country passed the 17th Amendment in 1913 and radically and fundamentally changed the structure of our government from a limited, federal institution to a national, all-powerful one. Though on paper the Constitution still reads as a grant to the federal government of limited, enumerated powers, the reality has become that, without the institutional check that state representation in the Senate provided, the federal government does as it pleases save for the extremely rare and almost extinct judicial check on its authority.

It is long past due for federalism to be restored and the 17th Amendment repealed. It is only by giving up the direct election of our senators can we ensure the return of a Constitution with teeth and a greater degree of liberty that is off-limits to Washington.

NULLIFICATION

(July 22, 2010)

Thomas Woods, author of a new book entitled Nullification: How to Resist Federal Tyranny in the 21st Century, spoke at the Celebrate the Constitution event held the Friday evening before the Iowa

Republican Party's State Convention. In his book, Woods argues that states have the sovereign right to actively resist and thwart unconstitutional federal laws such as ObamaCare.

The theory, first articulated by Thomas Jefferson in the Kentucky Resolutions of 1798, holds that the federal government "was not made the exclusive or final judges of the extent of the powers delegated to itself; since that would have made its discretion, and not the Constitution, the measure of its powers..."

Rather, according to what later became known as the "Spirit of '98," each state has an equal right to not only pass censure on a particular use of federal power, but also to determine "the mode and measure of redress." This sentiment was echoed by the Virginia Resolutions of 1798, drafted by James Madison.

The premise underlying the "Spirit of '98" is the compact theory—that, as Woods put it, "the United States [was] created by a group of independent political societies [i.e., the states] that established a federal government as their agent, reserving all undelegated powers to themselves[.]" Therefore, much as the principal is the master of the agent, so the states are the masters of their agent the federal government.

As evidence of state sovereignty, Woods argues that each state became an independent sovereign on July 4, 1776, when they declared their independence of Great Britain, and that this situation did not change under the Articles of Confederation. While this is true, Woods argues, as did Jefferson, Madison, and John C. Calhoun before him, that the Constitution itself did not change this but simply replaced the old treaty alliance of the Articles with a new one.

In short, nullification maintains that the federal government is a confederation government of sovereign states. This is a startling proposition, considering that 37 of the 50 states were created out of federal land by the federal government and, as a result, owe their existence to it. Certainly these states cannot be considered as sovereign states participating in a treaty league under the auspices of the Constitution. Because the federal government could, therefore, only be the agent of the original 13 states, the compact theory would create an unequal, two-tier system of states whereby the power of nullification belonged solely to those 13 states.

To buttress his argument of state sovereignty, Woods maintains that sovereignty is indivisible and, therefore, the original 13 states (after 1776) were unable to surrender their sovereignty to a national government, even if they had so desired. How is it, then, that Great Britain could surrender her sovereign claims to the colonies? Or that Native American tribes became semi-sovereign dependents of the federal government? Or that the United States could buy the Louisiana Purchase from France, who in turn had bought it from Spain?

Additionally, no where in his book does Woods examine the contrast between the compact theory in existence under the Articles of Confederation with the type of government bequeathed by the Constitution. Under the Articles, each state had one vote, regardless of population. The delegates of each state were completely dependent on the legislatures that selected them, paid them, instructed them how to vote, and could withdraw them at any time. Furthermore, the Congress under the Articles could only make resolutions, not enforce them.

Under the Constitution, however, the sates had equal representation in only one legislative chamber, the Senate. The President is chosen by electors, and Congressmen are elected by the people in districts that change after every decennial census. The elected officials of the new government are paid out of federal coffers, are free to ignore the instructions of the states, and cannot be recalled by them. And the laws of the federal government are declared to be the supreme law of the land and binding on state governments.

As many anti-federalists noted at the time, the Constitution replaced the multinational compact under the Articles with a national government of the people. The importance of this cannot be overstated, because under a government made up of sovereign states rather than We the People, only the states would have the right to amend it, to sue it, to engage in civil disobedience, or to rebel against it. Under the compact theory, since We the People are not parties to the federal government, we have no rights or claims against it even though it taxes and regulates us.

While we should amend the Constitution to allow, as Woods and others have proposed, for two-thirds of the states to be able to veto acts of Congress, the doctrine of nullification and the compact theory it represents has no basis in our Constitution.

CHECKING THE FEDERAL GOVERNMENT TOGETHER (August 2, 2010)

The recent discussion over nullification and the 10th Amendment has shown that there is a wide-spread desire for additional constitutional checks on the federal government. Many supporters of nullification are attracted to it, not necessarily because they understand or agree with the theory behind it, but because they see it as the only means of keeping Congress within its constitutional boundaries.

Much like an executive order staying court decisions, people see nullification as the means to control a government that they no longer feel any control over. Doubtless the Founders would have added additional checks and balances into the Constitution if they could have foreseen the rise of the modern social state controlled by Washington, but their failure does not justify us in reading our own remedies into the Constitution.

The desire for results, no matter how desirable, is no excuse for the use of power if that power is illegitimate. That is the hard task of the law, especially when that law is the fundamental will of the people expressed in a written Constitution. It is important, then, to understand whether or not our desired remedy has any constitutional authority before we seek to implement it. If it doesn't, then we should focus our energies on passing constitutional amendments that would legitimize effectual checks on federal authority.

As we put aside our desire for immediate, tangible results to honestly examine the issue of nullification, the very first question we encounter is whether the Constitution was formed by We the People or by the states. If it is formed by We the People, the states are not a party to this contract and have no more ability to interfere with federal laws than our local municipalities, school boards, or the UN.

If We the People formed the Constitution, then only we have the power to judge whether or not the federal government has overstepped the power we delegated to it and, if so, to elect new representatives, amend the Constitution, or engage in civil disobedience. However, if the states delegated some of their authority to the federal government, then they would have the sole right to judge whether or not that delegation has been usurped.

That the federal government was created by We the People rather than the states can be abundantly seen in the fact that federal officials are elected by the people and are uncontrollable by the states. Additionally, new states, though undoubtedly formed by the voters in each territory, enjoyed none of the traditional characteristics of a sovereign independent state and, therefore, were incapable of delegating any authority to the federal government.

But the most convincing evidence of all are the words of those who drafted and ratified the Constitution, which clearly demonstrate that it was an act of We the People rather than a compact of the states. In the years after the Constitution was ratified, individuals and states have advocated the theory of nullification and state's rights to stop overreaching by the federal government. But, no matter how laudable those efforts may have been, these acts and words spoken after the act of ratification are no more guides to interpreting the Constitution than ObamaCare and No Child Left Behind are.

The overwhelming evidence, therefore, is that We the People formed the Constitution, and consequently only we can be the judges of whether or not the federal government has overstepped the authority we delegated to it. The Tenth Amendment is subsequently irrelevant to this discussion because

We the People have taken from the states their authority as sovereign, independent states, including the power to interfere with our contract with the federal government.

As several of the state ratifying conventions made clear, only We the People have the power to resume the sovereign power we have delegated to the federal government if it oversteps its authority. It follows, then, that the power to nullify federal laws is simply not a reserved power under the Tenth Amendment because that amendment is incapable of reserving power to the states that they do not and cannot possess.

Since there is no constitutional authority for nullification, we must abandon our quest for an easy but illegitimate solution and focus our efforts on passing amendments to the Constitution that would enable us to better restrain the federal government within its constitutional straightjacket.

Though that may seem like an insurmountable hurdle, federal constitutional amendments tend to come in waves of two-to-five at a time, spurred on by a new generation adding its own addendum to the Constitution. The last such wave was in the 1960's, and it is time for another wave to provide two-thirds of the states with a veto over federal legislation, correct the misinterpretation of the Tax & Spend and Commerce Clauses, a balanced budget amendment, repealing the 16th (income tax) and 17th Amendments, provide for judicial term limits, establishing a temporary tay of court decisions, etc.

This discussion over nullification, began in good faith, was never intended as a "hit piece." Rather, its purpose was to encourage all who abhor the unconstitutional growth of the federal government to put our energies towards a common goal that we can all agree on.

We the People are the ultimate sovereigns, and the time is now for us to unite together to take aggressive steps via constitutional amendments to push the federal government back into its constitutional sphere. To that end, we need to elect state and federal officials who, rather than advocating for nullification, will work to pass such amendments to the U.S. Constitution.

AN UNCONSTITUTIONAL CONSTITUTION?

(November 10, 2010)

In a November 6th interview with Senator-Elect Mike Lee (R-UT) on his Freedom Watch program on the Fox Business Network, Judge Andrew Napolitano argued that part of the U.S. Constitution is itself unconstitutional. That provision, according to Napolitano, is the 17th Amendment, which removed the selection of U.S. Senators from the statehouse to direction election by the people. Napolitano argued that this amendment is the:

> Death knell of the idea that the federal government is a coming together of independent sovereign states. The 17th amendment meant that the States no longer had a place at the federal table along with the popularly elected House of Representatives and the President elected by the Electoral College. The very idea of the Constitution as an agreement among sovereign states has been assaulted. The 17th Amendment is the part of the Constitution that is unconstitutional and it should be repealed.

Napolitano has long been an advocate of the theory of state's rights, writing in his book The Constitution in Exile that: "[Abraham Lincoln] blatantly ignored the rights of the states to secede from the Union, a right that is clearly implicit in the Constitution, since it was the states that ratified the Constitution and thereby decided to enter the Union. Surely these same states had the right to decide to undo that act."

As has been previously noted, We the People rather than the States ratified the Constitution and, therefore, the States have no right to interfere in our contract by succession or nullification. But, even assuming that Napolitano is correct that the Constitution is a contract between sovereign States, that doesn't mean the 17th Amendment is constitutional for the simple reason that it was lawfully ratified pursuant to that contract.

Constitutional theory aside, Napolitano's larger point, shared by Senator-Elect Lee, is that, ideally, the 17th Amendment should be repealed. This is something that all constitutionalists can agree on. Because the Founding Generation knew that constitutional limits on federal power were simply parchment prohibitions, they devised institutional checks and balances in the structure of the federal government so that, as James Madison wrote, each of the "constituent parts may...be the means of keeping each other in their proper places."

But, as the last century has made abundantly clear, once the States lost their voice in the federal government, they become mere handmaidens of unrestrained national power and that federalism, that great preserver of the greatest amount of liberty for the American people, was reduced to a mere shadow of its constitutional self.

Any effort, however, to restore that voice to the States by repealing the 17th Amendment is dead upon arrival in Congress. As Senator-Elect Lee noted in his interview with Napolitano, "...in practical terms, I don't think it will be likely in our lifetime that there will be the political will to abolish the 17th Amendment."

Even if the 17th Amendment were repealed in the next few years, it would likely have little effect on how Washington does business. It may prevent unfunded federal mandates and some of the most obnoxious federal legislation such as ObamaCare and No Child Left Behind, but by itself it will do little to change a hundred-year-power-grab by Congress.

The answer, radical as it is, is simply for the Constitution to be enforced, first, by our federal legislators and, as a last resort, by our courts. With or without the 17th Amendment, the Constitution establishes a federal government of limited, enumerated powers.

Until the political will exists among We the People to demand that our elected officials begin to take incremental steps towards constitutional responsibility again, the repeal of the 17th Amendment will accomplish precious little.

Though on life-support ten, five, or even two years ago, there are signs that this political will is again stirring and growing in momentum as Americans read and study their Constitution.

The first test of the political power of this modern wave of constitutionalism will be to hold the Republicans to their Pledge to America in which they: "Pledge[d] to honor the Constitution as constructed by its framers and honor the original intent of those precepts that have been consistently ignored—particularly the Tenth Amendment."

The campaign may be over for Republicans as they move from being candidates to governing as a majority party in the House, but the campaign for constitutionally literate and responsible federal legislators has just begun.

NULLIFYING LEVIATHAN

(June 28, 2012)

The long, slow death of federalism is nearly complete. While perhaps an enthusiasm boost for the GOP heading into the November election, the Supreme Court's Obamacare decision is yet another nail in the coffin of a federal government of limited, enumerated powers. Since the Constitution has become all but a dead letter, it is time to empower the States against an unrestrained centralized government.

While a majority of the Court held that the Constitution's Commerce Clause did not authorize the individual mandate for individuals not currently in a commercial market, only Justice Thomas was willing to overturn any of the Court's existing caselaw that gives Congress extensive powers never imagined by the Founding Generation.

As Obamacare's opponents conceded at oral argument, Congress could, under Supreme Court precedent, "say [that], if you're going to consume health services, you have to pay by way of insurance." Rather than disturb this precedent, a majority of the Court simply refused to say that Congress could force you to purchase health insurance before entering the market instead of at the point of needing health care.

In essence, eight justices on the Supreme Court believe that Congress can impose all the mandates it wants on those already in commerce. For instance, Congress could mandate that home buyers buy mortgage insurance, or that existing car owners install antipollution devices, or that purchasers of new home windows buy energy efficient models. And Congress doesn't even have to call these fines taxes, because they are economic mandates under the Commerce Clause.

Congress does, however, have to call a mandate it places on individuals not participating in a particular market a tax. Congress can tax individuals to "encourage" them into doing whatever it wants, irrespective of any conceivable connection to one of its enumerated powers, so long as the tax does not become coercive. Though declining to specify when a tax becomes unconstitutionally punitive, the Court assures us that the "power to tax is not the power to destroy while this Court sits."

Noticeably, the Chief Justice was unable to explain how the mandate was not unduly punitive under Congress' taxing power while at the same time so punitive that it "compels" individuals into the market in violation of the Commerce Clause. Whatever the distinction, the practical effect is that Congress can do nearly whatever it pleases, either under its commerce power or its taxing power.

Some have suggested that it will be politically prohibitive for Congress to pass such mandates in the future if it has to acknowledge that they are, in fact, taxes. Though it is true that Obamacare would not have passed as a tax, it is entirely plausible that a less ambitious bill stripped of everything but the mandate to pay for coverage of preexisting conditions would have. Majorities have few quibbles with taxing the minority to get something "free."

Since the Court has refused to impose any real limits on federal authority, some have argued that the states should nullify Obamacare. Already two states, Ohio and Missouri, have passed state constitutional amendments nullifying the individual mandate, and approximately a dozen other states are considering joining North Dakota in doing so by simple legislation.

Unfortunately, nullification is based on an unsupported theory that the federal government is the creation of the states rather than We the People. In addition to the lack of historical or constitutional reality, such a theory misstates the nature of government.

As individual sovereigns, We the People initially delegated a portion of our sovereignty to the states for the mutual protection of our unalienable rights before the creation of the federal government. Consequently, only We the People could re-delegate some of that sovereignty from the states and give it to the federal government.

Because the states were without permission from We the People to re-delegate such powers, they were incapable of creating the federal government. Only We the People could, and did so at that state ratifying conventions. In doing so, however, we made no provision in the new constitution that would allow the states to nullify these re-delegated powers.

But We the People, as ultimate sovereigns who remain the judges of when the "consent of the governed" has been breached, can exercise our unalienable right of nullification at the state level, either by piece-meal constitutional amendments as the need arises (mandates, immigration, Roe, etc.), or by a constitutional amendment generally delegating such nullifying authority to the legislature.

Perhaps it is time to act as individual sovereigns again.

3 LIMITED, ENUMERATED POWERS

DOES THE CONSTITUTION STOP OBAMACARE?

(April 12, 2010)

When asked that question last fall, House Speaker Nancy Pelosi was temporarily caught off guard, finally sputtering, "Are you serious?" A few seconds later she gave the same response, "Are you serious?" She then quickly turned to another reporter without further comment. Another Democrat, Representative Phil Hare (IL), reacted similarly when recently posed that question by one of his constituents, "I don't really worry about the Constitution on this to be honest."

While the thought that the Constitution actually limited the power of Congress to enact legislation may be foreign to Democrats, the Constitution's Framers intended for the federal government to be one of limited powers that were specifically enumerated in the text of the document.

James Madison, writing in the Federalist Papers, wrote that, "The proposed Government cannot be deemed a national one; since its jurisdiction extends to certain enumerated objects only, and leaves to the several States a residuary and inviolable sovereignty over all other objects."

If the federal government is one of enumerated powers, than the power to regulate health care would have to be one of the powers specifically given to it in the Constitution. Out of the 17 named powers given to Congress in Section 8 of Article 1, however, none of them mentions anything about heath care, insurance, doctors, medical treatment, or anything approaching an enumerated power that would allow Congress to legislate our health.

Then how is it that Democrats can claim the Constitution permits their health care legislation? Democrats point to two constitutional provisions as their grant of authority to enact health care legislation.

The first enumerated power claimed by Democrats is the General Welfare Clause. House Majority Leader Steny Hoyer (D-Md), for instance, claimed that Congress has "broad authority" to provide for the general welfare. The term "general welfare" appears twice in the Constitution, once in the Preamble and another time in the Tax and Spend Clause.

The Preamble to the Constitution, however, has never been considered a grant of power to the federal government. As the Supreme Court has put it, "[a]lthough th[e] preamble indicates the general purposes for which the people ordained and established the Constitution, it has never been regarded as the source of any substantive power conferred on the government of the United States."

The Tax and Spend Clause, however, is an enumerated power given to Congress in the Constitution. It reads in part, "[t]he Congress shall have Power To lay and collect Taxes, Duties, Imposts and Excises, to pay the Debts and provide for the common Defence and general Welfare of the United States."

To read the term "general welfare" in the Clause to be a broad grant of authority to Congress to tax for whatever purposes it deems are in the general welfare of the country would be to make a mockery of the Constitution. Such a broad grant of authority would eclipse a written constitution of enumerated specific, limited powers given to the federal government.

As Thomas Jefferson explained, "the laying of taxes is the power, and the general welfare the purpose for which the power is to be exercised. [Congress is] not to lay taxes ad libitum for any purpose they please."

James Madison also noted that, "Such a view of the Constitution, finally, would have the effect of excluding the judicial authority of the United States from its participation in guarding the boundary between the legislative powers of the General and the State Governments, inasmuch as questions relating to the general welfare, being questions of policy and expediency, are unsusceptible of judicial cognizance and decision."

The second enumerated power Democrats claim supports their authority to regulate the health care industry is the Commerce Clause. The Constitution does in fact specifically give Congress the power "to regulate commerce with foreign nations, among the several states, and with the Indian tribes."

The Clause, however, was simply meant to prevent trade wars between the states, something that was a common occurrence under the Articles of Confederation. The inability of the Continental Congress to resolve trade disputes among the various states and with foreign nations was one of the leading reasons the states called for a new federal government.

Originally understood, the Commerce Clause was intended to create a "free trade zone" throughout America, only giving Congress the power to strike down state laws that discriminated against the buying, selling, and transportation of out-of-state goods.

Madison, in 1832, wrote that the Clause was "a necessary control on the conduct of some of the importing States towards their non-importing neighbors." Never once, in the Federalist Papers or the debates during the Constitution's ratification, did anyone suggest that the Commerce Clause was anything more than the power to eliminate trade barriers among the states.

Ever looking to expand its power, Congress, with the acquiescence of the Supreme Court, has long ago seized on the Clause as its authority to regulate pretty much every detail of our lives. The Supreme Court has gone so far as to uphold federal legislation that prohibited local, non-economic activity such as growing wheat or marijuana for personal consumption under the absurd theory that, since the home-grown product is used instead of that which is transported across state lines, it has an effect on interstate commerce. Such a theory, however, transforms the federal government into one with unlimited powers.

But the health care legislation goes even further than what the Court has previously upheld by requiring an individual person to engage in economic transaction with a private company (i.e., buy health insurance) or face a fine. That is an unprecedented and unconstitutional power grab by Congress that, if upheld, would leave no check on Congress' power. The concept of federalism and limited government would be dead.

It is time for the Supreme Court to once again hold that the Constitution imposes restrictions on Congress and to close the General Welfare and Commerce Clause expressways by which the federal government has become one of infinite powers rather than finite authority.

NO TAXATION WITHOUT REPRESENTATION, UNLESS YOU LIKE YOUR GUNS

(April 22, 2010)

This past Thursday, the U.S. House of Representatives had intended to debate the District of Columbia Voting Rights Acts but, thankfully, never did. The reason was not concern over the doubtful constitutionality of the measure, but rather the Democrats unwillingness to grant D.C. residents their gun rights. Just last week President Obama had urged Congress to pass the Act by November, a deadline that now seems improbable.

In a conference with reporters on Tuesday, House Majority Leader Steny Hoyer (D-MD) broke the news that the bill would not be debated this week. He stated that, though he was "profoundly disappointed," the legislation would be indefinitely tabled, because "[t]he price was too high."

What price? The Republicans added an amendment to the bill that would force the District of Columbia to lax its gun laws, which still remain among the strictest in the nation even after the Supreme Court found portions of the regulations unconstitutional in D.C. v. Heller.

The Democrats were unwilling to force a vote on the issue, which would likely have ruptured the party between its liberal establishment and its more conservative members from suburban and rural America.

The bill would have added two seats in the House, one for the heavily-Democratic District of Columbia (which currently has a non-voting member) and the other would be a temporary at-large seat for predominately Republican Utah, which had narrowly missed out on getting another seat after the 2000 census.

The rallying cry for those in favor of giving the District of Columbia voting rights is the tried and true "no taxation without representation." While that truism strikes a cord with Americans now as much as it did in 1776, Congress cannot simply grant voting rights to those who do not reside in a state.

The Constitution specifically provides in Article 1, Section 8 that the seat of the federal government is to be located in a "District (not exceeding ten miles square) as may, by cession of particular states, and the acceptance of Congress..."

The reason the Founders wanted the capital to be placed in a federal territory was to prevent it from being dependent on the good graces (or blackmail) of a particular state for its security and economic well-being.

Because the District was a federal territory, its residents originally could not vote for a president because Article 2, Section 1 limited that right to states. It was not until the 23rd Amendment that an exception was made for the District of Columbia, though exceptions were not also carved out for residents of other federal territories such as Guam and Puerto Rico.

Similarly, Article 1, Section 2 provides that "[t]he House of Representatives shall be composed of

Members chosen every second Year by the People of the several States." (emphasis added) Recognizing that it would take a constitutional amendment to give the District the right to a representative, both the House and the Senate passed one in 1978 but it failed to be ratified by three-fourths of the states.

Supporters of the legislation claim that, despite this, Congress can still give the District of Columbia a representative by the ordinary legislative process because Article 1, Section 8 grants it the power of "exclusive legislation" over the District.

But Congress itself, by passing these two constitutional amendments (one successful and the other not), recognized that this grant of authority was insufficient to change the clear text of the Constitution. If it was, Congress would, at least in the District, be supreme over the Constitution and unfettered in its power. Clearly this was not what the Founders had in mind by "exclusive legislation."

While it may be an idea past due to give residents of D.C. the right to vote for a Congressman, it should only be done by a constitutional amendment and in a manner, like the 23rd Amendment, which continues to preserve the District's unique position as a federal territory.

IS THE CONSTITUTION A PAPER TIGER?
(May 23, 2010)

Recently, the U.S. Supreme Court ruled in U.S. v. Comstock (2010) that the federal government can civilly commit, indefinitely, those deemed "sexually dangerous" when their federal prison sentences are complete. Not surprisingly, those facing such civil commitments claimed that the statute overstepped Congress' constitutional authority.

Contrary to the belief of many members of Congress of both parties, the Constitution does impose limits on what they can and cannot do. They have very specific enumerated powers under the Constitution, and those not granted to the federal government are, as the Tenth Amendment exhorts, "reserved to the States respectively, or to the people."

The powers given to the Congress are not only specific, but also quite limited—the ability to borrow money, establish currency and punish counterfeiting, provide for patents and copyrights, declare war, organize the militias, etc. In fact, the Framers were initially of the opinion that a Bill of Rights was unnecessary because they believed Congress did not have the power to reach those rights.

This is the meaning of federalism—the simple and fundamental proposition that the federal government has only a few, specific powers and cannot exercise any that are not "necessary and proper" to those enumerated powers. Though it may be unpopular to habitually tell the federal government "NO," especially when the laws are desirable, the Constitution itself is a document of "NOs," commanding the federal government that it may go this far but no further.

The first question every congressmen, president, and judge must ask of a piece of legislation is not whether it is popular or whether it is the right thing to do, but whether the Constitution allows it. If it is not an exercise of one of the specific, enumerated powers found in the Constitution, they must next ask if it is "necessary and proper" to the execution of one of those powers.

In this case, the answer to the first question is simple—civilly committing dangerous individuals is not an enumerated power found in the Constitution. In fact, no where does the Constitution give Congress the power to enact a general criminal code or provide for civil commitments of dangerous or mentally ill individuals.

The second question, then, is whether the legislation is a means of executing one of Congress' enumerated powers. For instance, Congress can define crimes that interfere with its constitutionally-delegated power of regulating the post office. Or it can define crimes that interfere with its enumerated power to grant patents and copyrights, or its power to tax, or its power to raise and support armies.

But there aren't any enumerated powers that civil commitments are meant to help execute. Not even Solicitor General Elena Kagan, now nominated by President Obama to the Supreme Court, was able at oral arguments to identify any conceivable enumerated power that this piece of legislation was intended to help implement.

Rather, General Kagan argued, and the Court bought, the theory that Congress has the power to enact the statute because it was, in their opinion, rationally related to another law which did implement an enumerated power. In other words, because Congress had the power to imprison these individuals for an offense under one of its enumerated powers, the Court also held it had the power to determine which were too dangerous to release back into the public.

But the Constitution's requirement that federal laws be "necessary and proper" does not allow Congress to pass legislation that furthers other federal laws. Rather, the proper question is whether the challenged law itself is enacted to further an enumerated power. For instance, laws defining federal offenses, determining the punishment, and regulating the confinement of prisoners are all means of carrying out a specifically granted power.

As an example, because Congress has the power to establish post offices, it can pass a law criminalizing the theft of mail. Because Congress has the power to establish post offices, it can make the theft of mail punishable by five years in prison. Because Congress has the power to establish post offices, it can make theft of mail punishable by five years in prison at a minimum-security prison.

But civilly confining "sexually dangerous" predators is not a means of executing an enumerated power, but a means of protecting the general public from degenerates. Congress cannot say, "Because we have such and such enumerated power, we can throw away the keys on sexually dangerous people." There is no "such and such" power enumerated in the Constitution to give them that authority, no matter how laudable it may be to protect society from sexual deviants.

To be constitutional, a federal law must be a means of executing a constitutionally enumerated power rather than simply having a casual link to another federal law. Otherwise, by a series of stepping stones in which laws are passed because they have some relationship with other federal laws, the Constitution becomes a grant of general authority rather than limited power.

Ruefully, the majority of the Court in failed to enforce these constitutional roadblocks on Congress' power, leaving that body free to legislate as it pleases and turning the doctrine of enumerated powers into a paper tiger.

ABOLISHING THE DEPARTMENT OF EDUCATION?

(June 12, 2010)

Sharron Angle, the Tea Party favorite who won the Republican Senate nomination in Nevada, has been labeled an extremist for, among other things, wanting to abolish the federal department of education. The Department of Education was signed into law in 1979 by President Jimmy Carter. At the time, however, the new department was criticized by members of the president's own party.

"No matter what anyone says, the Department of Education will not just write checks to local school boards. They will meddle in everything. I do not want that," argued Representative Pat Schroeder (D-CO). Representative Joseph Early (D-MA) stated that a "national Department may actually impede the innovation of local programs as it attempts to establish uniformity throughout the Nation."

Senator Patrick Moynihan (D-NY) condemned the new law as a straight political payoff by Carter to teacher unions for their endorsement in the 1976 presidential election. "This is a back-room deal, born out of squalid politics. Everything we had thought we would not see happening to education is happening here."

For many years after its creation, abolishing the Department was a staple among Republican politicians. Ronald Reagan famously pledged to abolish it in the 1980 presidential election, and even such Republicans in Name Only (RINOs) as John McCain supported cutting the Department during the Republican Revolution of 1994.

As late as 1996, the Republican Party platform stated: "The Federal government has no constitutional authority to be involved in school curricula or to control jobs in the market place. This is why we will abolish the Department of Education." But then came President George W. Bush and No Child Left Behind, which grew the Department by 69.6 percent in just two years.

While there are very good policy reasons why the Department should be abolished, an even stronger argument can be made that Congress just doesn't have the constitutional authority to either fund or regulate education. Among the limited and enumerated powers given to Congress in Article 1, section 8 of the Constitution, not one of them has anything to do with education.

In establishing the Department, Congress attempted to explain its constitutional basis as follows: "The Congress declares that the establishment of a Department of Education is in the public interest, will promote the general welfare of the United States, will help ensure that education issues receive proper treatment at the Federal level, and will enable the Federal Government to coordinate its education activities more effectively."

None of those bases, however, can be found in the text of the Constitution itself. Congress' reasons are quite similar to the Preamble to the Constitution, which reads: "We the people of the United States, in order to form a more perfect Union, establish justice, insure domestic Tranquility, provide for the common defense, promote the general Welfare, and secure the Blessings of Liberty to ourselves and our Posterity, do ordain and establish this Constitution for the United States of America."

As the Supreme Court noted in Jacobson v. Massachusetts (1905), "[a]lthough that Preamble indicates the general purposes for which the people ordained and established the Constitution, it has never been regarded as the source of any substantive power conferred on the Government of the United States or on any of its Departments." The reason for this is simple—if the Preamble itself were a grant of power, it would have been pointless for the Framers to follow that all-encompassing grant of power with a constitution of limited and well-defined powers.

The Tax and Spend Clause of Article 1, Section 8, does provide that "Congress shall have Power To lay and collect Taxes, Duties, Imposts and Excises, to pay the Debts and provide for the common Defence and general Welfare of the United States."

But, as with the Preamble, to read the term "general welfare" in this clause to be a broad grant of authority to Congress to tax for whatever purposes it deems would eclipse a written constitution of specific, limited powers given to the federal government. Congress only has the power to tax and spend in furtherance of its limited constitutional powers, of which education is not one of them.

Instead of being criticized, Sharron Angle should be applauded for having the guts as a candidate for elected office to say "no." As unfortunately too many other politicians have discovered, it is all too easy to tell the electorate "yes we can" to win elections rather than, as the Constitution clearly states, "no we can't."

FEDERAL FUNDING FOR STEM CELL RESEARCH?
(August 29, 2010)

Recently, U.S. District Court Judge Royce Lamberth, sitting on the federal trial court in Washington, D.C., issued a preliminary ruling that federal funding could not be used for research on human embryonic stem cells. On August 9, 2001, President George W. Bush had prohibited the use of federal funding for research on embryonic stem cells created after his policy went into effect, though such funds were available for preexisting cell lines.

President Obama lifted that ban on March 9, 2009, in order to, in his words, "enhance the contribution of America's scientists to important new discoveries and new therapies for the benefit of humankind." Judge Lamberth found this executive order to violate the Dickey-Wicker Amendment, a rider to the Balanced Budget Downpayment Act of 1996.

The Dickey-Wicker Amendment, which has been included in every appropriation bill for the Department of Health and Human Services since 1996, prohibits the use of federal funds for "(1) the creation of a human embryo or embryos for research purposes; or (2) research in which a human embryo or embryos are destroyed, discarded, or knowingly subjected to risk of injury or death greater than that allowed for research on fetuses in utero under" applicable federal regulations.

Ruling that, in passing the Dickey-Wicker Amendment, Congress had prohibited the use of federal funds for researching embryonic stem cells, Judge Lamberth issued a preliminary injunction enjoining President Obama's executive order. The court did not hold that Congress could not provide such funding; only that it had specifically decided not to and the President is therefore bound by that decision.

But in doing so, however, Judge Lamberth overlooked the initial, fundamental question every judge (and politician) must ask—does the federal government have the power to do what it is attempting to do. In other words, with or without the

Dickey-Wicker Amendment, does the federal government have the power to fund embryonic stem cell research? This essential, basic question has been lost in the debate over the media acclaim for the desirability of such research, or at least the promised results it is supposed to yield.

The answer is clear and unambiguous—the federal government does not have the constitutional authority to spend money on stem cell research, or any medical research of any kind. Even if there was universal consensus that such funding was moral and appropriate, Congress lacks the power under the Constitution to do anything about it.

In Federalist No. 39, James Madison wrote: "[T]he proposed Government cannot be deemed a national one; since its jurisdiction extends to certain enumerated objects only, and leaves to the several States a residuary and inviolable sovereignty over all other objects."

Because the federal government is composed of - and constrained by - enumerated powers, then the power to fund medical science would have to be one of the powers specifically given to it in the Constitution. But out of the seventeen named powers given to Congress in Section 8 of Article 1, none mention anything about medicine, science, health care, or anything else approaching an enumerated power that would allow Congress to provide for federal funding of stem cell research.

Doubtless, proponents of such funding will argue that Congress has broad authority to spend for the "general welfare" under the Congress' enumerated tax and spend power. The Tax and Spend Clause reads in part, "[T]he Congress shall have Power To lay and collect Taxes, Duties, Imposts and Excises, to pay the Debts and provide for the common Defence and general Welfare of the United States."

But to read the term "general welfare" in the clause to be a broad grant of authority to Congress to tax for whatever purposes it deems are in the general welfare of the country would be to make a mockery of the Constitution. Such a broad grant of authority would eclipse a written constitution of enumerated specific, limited powers given to the federal government.

As Thomas Jefferson explained, "[T]he laying of taxes is the power, and the general welfare the purpose for which the power is to be exercised. [Congress is] not to lay taxes ad libitum for any purpose they please."

Madison also noted: "Such a view of the Constitution, finally, would have the effect of excluding the judicial authority of the United States from its participation in guarding the boundary between the legislative powers of the General and the State Governments, inasmuch as questions relating to the general welfare, being questions of policy and expediency, are unsusceptible of judicial cognizance and decision."

Rather than simply holding that President Obama's executive order violated the Dickey-Wicker Amendment, Judge Lamberth should have gone back to first principles and ruled that the federal government was utterly without constitutional authority to authorizing such funding even if it had wanted to.

STRICT CONSTRUCTIONIST POLITICIANS
(September 17, 2010)

Constitution Day is celebrated on September 17th, the day on which 223 years ago the Constitutional Convention meeting in Philadelphia signed the Constitution and submitted it to the states for ratification. Delaware became the first state to ratify the Constitution a few months later on December 7th. It wasn't until the Constitution was ratified by the ninth state, New Hampshire, on June 21, 1788 that it went into effect.

In the formative years of our early Republic, members of Congress actually deliberated on the extent of their constitutional authority. Serious and thoughtful debates were had over whether or not Congress could build canals, subsidize cod fishers, give money to refugees of insurrections in San Domingo, or establish a national bank.

Whether or not something was constitutional was extremely important to the generation that gave birth to our country. Most politicians today, however, lack even a rudimentary understanding of the Constitution or the restraints it places on their power.

For instance, when asked last fall where the Constitution permits Congress to require citizens to buy health insurance, House Speaker Nancy Pelosi was temporarily caught off guard, finally sputtering, "Are you serious? Are you serious?" She then quickly turned to another reporter without further comment.

Another Democrat, Rep. Phil Hare of Illinois, reacted similarly when recently posed that question by one of his constituents: "I don't really worry about the Constitution on this, to be honest."

But the first requirement of every member of Congress is to worry about the Constitution and whether it gives them the power to enact the contemplated legislation. Unlike state governments which generally have widespread authority to regulate, the federal government is made up of limited, enumerated power.

As James Madison noted in Federalist No. 45, "The powers delegated by the proposed Constitution to the federal government are few and defined. Those which are to remain in the State governments are numerous and indefinite." To make his point, Madison asked rhetorically in Federalist No. 41, "For what purpose could the enumeration of particular powers be inserted, if these and all others were meant to be included in the preceding general power?"

Alexander Hamilton argued in Federalist No. 84 that a Bill of Rights was unnecessary because the federal government did not possess the power to interfere with any rights in the first place. "[A] minute detail of particular rights is certainly far less applicable to a Constitution like that under consideration, which is merely intended to regulate the general political interests of the nation, than to a constitution which has the regulation of every species of personal and private concerns."

He went on to argue that, by enumerating specific rights in a Bill of Rights, the argument could be made that the people felt they were necessary precisely because the federal government possessed the power to infringe them. "I go further, and affirm that bills of rights, in the sense and to the extent in which they are contended for, are not only unnecessary in the proposed Constitution, but would even be dangerous. They would contain various exceptions to powers not granted; and, on this very account, would afford a colorable pretext to claim more than were granted.

"For why declare that things shall not be done which there is no power to do? Why, for instance, should it be said that the liberty of the press shall not be restrained, when no power is given by which restrictions may be imposed? I will not contend that such a provision would confer a regulating power; but it is evident that it would furnish, to men disposed to usurp, a plausible pretense for claiming that power."

These limited, enumerated powers given to Congress are found in Section 8 of Article 1 of the

Constitution, and to refresh the memory of our federal legislators they are as follows:

1. The Congress shall have power To lay and collect Taxes, Duties, Imposts and Excises, to pay the Debts and provide for the common Defence and general Welfare of the United States; but all Duties, Imposts and Excises shall be uniform throughout the United States;

2. To borrow money on the credit of the United States;

3. To regulate Commerce with foreign Nations, and among the several States, and with the Indian Tribes;

4. To establish a uniform Rule of Naturalization, and uniform Laws on the subject of Bankruptcies throughout the United States;

5. To coin Money, regulate the Value thereof, and of foreign Coin, and fix the Standard of Weights and Measures;

6. To provide for the Punishment of counterfeiting the Securities and current Coin of the United States;

7. To establish Post Offices and Post Roads;

8. To promote the Progress of Science and useful Arts, by securing for limited Times to Authors

and Inventors the exclusive Right to their respective Writings and Discoveries;

9. To constitute Tribunals inferior to the Supreme Court;

10. To define and punish Piracies and Felonies committed on the high Seas, and Offenses against the Law of Nations;

11. To declare War, grant Letters of Marque and Reprisal, and make Rules concerning Captures on Land and Water;

12. To raise and support Armies, but no Appropriation of Money to that Use shall be for a longer Term than two Years;

13. To provide and maintain a Navy;

14. To make Rules for the Government and Regulation of the land and naval Forces;

15. To provide for calling forth the Militia to execute the Laws of the Union, suppress Insurrections and repel Invasions;

16. To provide for organizing, arming, and disciplining the Militia, and for governing such Part of them as may be employed in the Service of the United States, reserving to the States respectively, the Appointment of the Officers, and the Authority of training the Militia according to the discipline prescribed by Congress;

17. To exercise exclusive Legislation in all Cases whatsoever, over such District (not exceeding ten Miles square) as may, by Cession of particular States, and the acceptance of Congress, become the Seat of the Government of the United States, and to exercise like Authority over all Places purchased by the Consent of the Legislature of the State in which the Same shall be, for the Erection of Forts, Magazines, Arsenals, dock-Yards, and other needful Buildings.

For many years now, Republican politicians have clamored for strict constructionalist judges to be appointed to the federal bench. As laudable as such a goal is, perhaps we should first be seeking strict constructionalist politicians to serve in Congress. Long before questions over the constitutionality of federal legislation reach the Supreme Court, Congressmen should have wrestled with such questions themselves and be prepared to provide the Court, and their constituents, with their defense.

Though the process will not be easy or quick, We the People have the obligation to elect constitutionally responsible candidates.

CAN CONGRESS REGULATE CAMPAIGN FINANCE?
(September 15, 2010)

The short answer is yes, but only in the District of Columbia and other federal territories where the federal government has the authority to regulate for the general welfare much like state governments do in their jurisdictions. But outside of that quite limited exception, Congress is without the specific, enumerated power to regulate money in federal elections.

While much of the contention over federal campaign finance regulations have focused on First Amendment rights, such a debate wrongly concedes that Congress has the power to regulate in this area so long as it refrains from infringing on free speech. Rather, the very first question every piece of legislation must satisfy is whether or not Congress was granted the constitutional power to enact it.

The stated purpose of federal campaign finance laws is to "reform the financing of campaigns for election to Federal office" in order to prevent the "corruption and the appearance of corruption" in government and "equalize the relative ability of all citizens to affect the outcomes of elections." As laudable as that goal may be, a disputed proposition,

Congress simply does not have the power to pursue it.

Congress does have the power, under Section 4 of Article 1 of the Constitution, to "make or alter" state laws regulating the "times, places and manner of holding Elections for Senators and Representatives." The point of this provision was to provide for uniformity throughout the country as to the actual act of casting a ballot, and was intended to prevent the states from preventing federal elections from taking place.

As Alexander Hamilton noted in Federalist No. 60, it did not even include the power to regulate the "qualifications of the persons who may choose [i.e., the franchise] or be chosen [i.e., candidates]." If it did, Congress could have simply extended the franchise to blacks, women, and eighteen-to-twenty-year-olds without the need to pass the Fifteenth, Nineteenth and Twenty-Sixth Amendments, respectfully.

The Supreme Court, in Newberry v. United States (1921), struck down a federal campaign finance law because "we find no support in reason or authority for the argument that because the officers were created by the Constitution, Congress has some indefinite, undefined power over elections for

Senators and Representatives not derived from [Article i] Section 4."

The justices noted that Congress' authority over the time, place, and manner of Congressional elections did not extend to those things that are "prerequisites to elections or [that] may affect their outcomes—voters, education, means of transportation, health, public discussion, immigration, private animosities, even the face and figure of the candidate..." If the Constitution actually granted Congress such a power, the justices wrote, "[t]he history of the times indicate beyond a reasonable doubt that...it would not have been ratified."

The Court stressed that Congress could, under regulating the manner of actually casting a ballot, prevent voter fraud and intimidation. Additionally, it "should not be forgotten that, exercising inherent police power, the state may suppress whatever evils may be incident to primary or convention" or general election.

Finally, Article 1, Section 5 of the Constitution states that "each house shall be the judge of the elections, qualifications and returns of its own members." Congress can, as it famously did in the case of Congressman Adam Powell, Jr. (the man who preceded Charlie Rangel and whose son wants to succeed him), refuse to seat a Senator or Representative it believes is corrupt. The Court concluded, therefore, that "the national government is not without power to protect itself against corruption, fraud, or other malign influences."

In addition to its limited ability to regulate the actual act of voting for senators and representatives, Congress has the extremely narrow authority under Article II, Section 1 to "determine the time of choosing the [presidential] electors and the day on which they shall give their votes; and which day shall be the same throughout the United States."

That's it—the only power Congress has over presidential elections is picking the day. Article II, Section 1 expressly entrusts the manner of presidential elections to the exclusive jurisdiction of the states, and the place ("meet in their respective states") is specified by the Twelfth Amendment. This was understood by the Supreme Court in McPherson v. Blacker (1892), which held that "the appointment and mode of appointment of electors belong exclusively to the states under the constitution of the United States"

In short, the power to regulate money in politics, if it is to be exercised at all, belongs with the states. The federal government has no authority in this area at all, and it is past due for both Congress and the courts to reaffirm this.

THE IRS AND CHURCHES
(October 5, 2010)

Recently, Pastor Cary Gordon of Cornerstone World Outreach in Sioux City wrote a letter to other pastors to urge them to encourage their congregations to vote against retaining the three Supreme Court justices who are on the November ballot. These justices participated in the unanimous Iowa Supreme Court ruling last year that overturned Iowa's Defense of Marriage Act.

In his September 3rd letter, Gordon asks his fellow pastors "to commit to confront the injustice and ungodly decisions of the Iowa Supreme Court by boldly calling upon their flocks to 'vote no on judicial retention' for the three consecutive Sundays prior to Election Day."

Recognizing that this could jeopardize a church's tax-exempt status under IRS regulations, Gordon assures participating pastors that the Christian non-profit law firm "Liberty Institute will defend any courageous pastor or priest in the state of Iowa (from the IRS)—in court—for free—that is willing to follow the example of the New Testament church fathers who challenged the unscriptural public policies of their day as an example for every generation to follow."

This letter found its way into the hands of Americans United for Separation of Church and State, who in turn reported it to the Internal Revenue Service. Rev. Barry Lynn, the executive director of Americans United, said that "I don't think I have ever seen a more outrageous effort to politicize churches." Belying his true agenda, Lynn went on to say that it's "even more appalling that they are doing so in a bigoted attempt to deny civil rights to a targeted minority."

On Jan Mickelson's morning radio show Tuesday, Gordon stated that he looked forward to a confrontation with the IRS, hoping to take the case all the way up to the U.S. Supreme Court if need be to win the free speech rights of pastors. IRS regulations prohibit churches and other charitable organizations formed under section 501(c)(3) from endorsing or opposing candidates for elected office.

Supporters of the regulation argue that it is not a free speech issue at all. Rather, they maintain that the federal government is well within its right to define, for purposes of granting tax exempt status, what constitutes charitable activity. Accordingly, churches and other organizations are perfectly free to influence political elections as they desire, but if they wish not to be taxed by the federal government they have to play by its rules.

The problem with that, however, is that the federal government lacks the authority to use its taxing power to regulate matters outside its constitutional jurisdiction. This issue is not so much a free speech issue as it is a federalism issue—the federal government cannot do indirectly through its taxing power what it cannot do directly through one of its enumerated powers.

Under the Tax and Spend Clause, Congress has the authority to tax and spend "to pay the debts and provide for the common defense and general welfare." Traditionally, the term "general welfare" was understood to be shorthand for the remainder of Congress' powers which are listed immediately following the Clause.

Since the New Deal Era, however, Congress has read the term "general welfare" to mean pretty much whatever its heart desires. At this point in time, the political pressure is too great to spend federal money that it is unrealistic to hope that Congress would go back to the term's original public understanding.

It is not too much to hope, however, that Congress would once again recognize a few common sense limited restrictions on its tax and spend power, most of which have, at one time or another, been recognized by the courts.

The first restriction is that Congress cannot spend money on earmarked projects that circumvent otherwise applicable merit-based or competitive allocation processes because such earmarks violate the principle of national general welfare. The term "general welfare" means nothing if congressmen are allowed to earmark federal monies for specific projects rather than allocate the funding through an open process available nationwide.

The second is that Congress cannot impose upon state or local governments any obligation or duty to make expenditures unless such expenditures shall be fully reimbursed by the federal government.

Third, and perhaps most important but also most difficult to comply with, Congress lacks the constitutional authority to use its tax and spend power to regulate or prohibit any object or activity that is not necessary and proper to a power enumerated in the Constitution. It can spend money on those objects, but it is powerless to regulate them. Such regulations are left up to the States.

These are a few basic limitations on federal authority to tax and spend that would continue to allow states and the American people to feed at the trough of federal monies but also restore some resemblance of a federal government of limited, enumerated powers.

In this case, the federal government has used its tax and spend power to create an entire regulatory scheme of what non-profits—under either 501(c)(3), 501(c)(4), or section 527—can say and do. This is a clear violation of even the minimum constitutional restrictions described above because it attempts to regulate an area not entrusted to it by the Constitution.

While we may acquiescence in Congress' decision to promote charities by giving them a tax break even though promoting charity is not a constitutionally enumerated power, it cannot take the additional step and attach strings to its tax break. This is a power denied to Congress by the Constitution, and congressmen who are serious about being faithful to that document should seek to repeal these regulations.

UNCONSTITUTIONALLY PRO-LIFE
(June 19, 2011)

In an act of contradiction that has yet to be adequately explained, five Republican presidential hopefuls recently pledged to appoint originalists judges who would strike down as unconstitutional the federal fetal pain bill these candidates simultaneously pledged to "advance and sign." And though two of these five candidates currently serve in Congress, they have yet to introduce the legislation.

Congresswoman Michele Bachmann, former Speaker Newt Gingrich, Congressman Ron Paul, former Minnesota Governor Tim Pawlenty, and former Senator Rick Santorum all signed the Susan B. Anthony List (SBA List) Pro-Life Presidential Leadership Pledge, in which they pledge that, if elected, they will:

> One, only nominate to the U.S. federal bench judges who are committed to restraint and applying the original meaning of the Constitution, not legislating from the bench;
>
> Two, select only pro-life appointees for relevant Cabinet and Executive Branch positions,

> in particular the head of National Institutes of Health, the Department of Justice, and the Department of Health & Human Services;
>
> Three, advance pro-life legislation to permanently end all taxpayer funding of abortion in all domestic and international spending programs, and defund Planned Parenthood and all other contractors and recipients of federal funds with affiliates that perform or fund abortions;
>
> Four, advance and sign into law a Pain-Capable Unborn Child Protection Act to protect unborn children who are capable of feeling pain from abortion.

Both SBA List and Operation Rescue confirmed to The Iowa Republican (TIR) that the federal Pain-Capable Unborn Child Protection Act does not yet exist. Steve Valentine, the interim Legislative Outreach Director at SBA List, told TIR that they did not have any model legislation publicly available, but that the bill would roughly follow the fetal pain legislation passed by Nebraska in 2010.

Valentine told TIR that they are waiting for the "right political climate" to introduce the legislation, which he defined as a Republican-controlled White House, Senate, and House. Both Congresswoman Bachmann and Congressman Paul declined to respond to requests by TIR as to whether they would introduce or at least co-sponsor the Act in the House this year. So much for their pledge to "advance" the bill.

When asked the same question, Fred Love, Congressman Latham's spokesman, replied that: "Since this is not yet a federal bill, Congressman Latham is not able to signify support or opposition until he can review specific and finalized language. However, as a pro-life legislator, Congressman Latham is most certainly supportive of any proposal that has these merits." Congressman Latham's office declined to clarify his position when TIR attempted to follow up this non-answer by again specifically asking if he would introduce the bill himself.

In an interview with TIR earlier this week, Congressman King said that he was very supportive of the measure at both the state and federal level because we "understand medically that unborn children experience pain." He stated that he would look into introducing the Act if he concludes he would be the best person to do so, and hopes to come to a decision relatively soon. Senator Grassley declined to respond to TIR's inquiries.

Left unsatisfactorily answered by any of the five signatories of the Pledge or by Iowa's congressional delegation is which of Congress' enumerated powers provides the authority for the Act. The Pain-Capable Unborn Child Awareness Act pending in the Senate, for instance, appears to rely on Congress' authority to regulate interstate commerce to require that abortion providers inform mothers that their unborn child may feel pain after twenty weeks of gestation.

Given that an abortion occurs entirely within a single state, however, that enumerated power is inapplicable even under the Supreme Court's "lax (but not-infinite) version of the interstate commerce power." As Congressman Paul noted with regards to the 2003 Partial Birth Abortion Bill, "This greatly stretches the definition of interstate commerce. The abuse of both the interstate commerce clause and the general welfare clause is precisely the reason our federal government no longer conforms to constitutional dictates but, instead, balloons out of control in its growth and scope. [This bill] inadvertently justifies federal government intervention into every medical procedure through the gross distortion of the interstate commerce clause."

In contrast, the Life at Conception Act pending in the House, co-sponsored by Congressman King but not by Congresswoman Bachmann or Congressmen Paul and Latham, states as its constitutional basis: "To implement equal protection for the right to life of each born and preborn human person, and pursuant to the duty and authority of the Congress, including Congress' power under article I, section 8, to make necessary and proper laws, and Congress' power under section 5 of the 14th article of amendment to the Constitution of the United States, the Congress hereby declares that the right to life guaranteed by the Constitution is vested in each human being."

Congress has, under the 14th Amendment, the power to prevent States from "depriv[ing] any person of life, liberty, or property, without due process of law." The problem with applying "person" or "life" in this clause to the unborn is that the provision "simply requires that the law be followed before the government could execute a criminal, jail an individual, impose a fine, deprive a person of their estate, sentence them to exile, etc. The only right granted by this Clause was process—requiring the government to proceed according to the law of the land (i.e., constitutional and statutory provisions)."

Presumably recognizing this, the Life at Conception Act instead appears to claim as justification Congress' power under the 14th Amendment to prevent a State from "deny[ing] to any person...the equal protection of the laws." In other words, the Act holds that it is a violation of equal protection for the States to create laws punishing the murder of born persons differently than the murder of unborn persons.

Among other problems with this theory is that, as then-Justice William Rehnquist noted in his dissent in Roe v. Wade, "by the time of the adoption of the Fourteenth Amendment in 1868, there were at least thirty-six laws enacted by state or territorial legislatures limiting abortion." No one suggested during the ratification debates that these thirty-six laws would become unconstitutional because they did not outlaw the murder of all unborn children, nor did any State feel constitutionally-compelled to enact a blanket ban on abortions following ratification.

The Pain-Capable Unborn Child Protection Act appears, therefore, to be beyond the reach of Congress' enumerated powers. Unfortunately, Congresswoman Bachmann, Speaker Gingrich, and Governor Pawlenty all declined to explain to TIR why they would appoint originalist judges while at the same time "advance and sign" legislation that violates the original public understanding of the Constitution. Congressman Latham's office also declined to explain which enumerated power he would cite for congressional action, while Congressman King told TIR that the Interstate Commerce Clause would likely give Congress the authority, though he cautioned he would have to look closely at this issue.

Bachmann's silence is particularly odd, given that she, along with Ron Paul, co-sponsored the Enumerated Powers Act which would require that "each Act of Congress shall contain a concise and definite statement of the constitutional authority relied upon for the enactment of each portion of that Act." Proclaiming herself to be a constitutional conservative, she also quotes the Republican Pledge to America for the proposition that: "We pledge to honor the Constitution as constructed by its framers and honor the original intent of those precepts that have been consistently ignored..."

Senator Santorum did respond to TIR inquiries, stating that "I do not believe the protection of innocent life violates originalist understandings of the Constitution, period. Indeed, I believe the Constitution is meaningless if innocent life is considered unprotected." This is no more convincing than saying one believes the Constitution is meaningless if "marriage equality is considered unprotected," or "millions of Americans are without affordable health insurance," or "there are starving kids in the street." Declaring something an important virtue does not transform it into a federally constitutionally-enumerated end.

Congressman Paul, who recently declared that "I can defend everything I do by the Constitution," told TIR that, while the "Pain-Capable Unborn Child Protection Act is not perfect legislation...I would sign the Unborn Child Protection Act and encourage my fellow pro-life leaders to vote for it. I voted for the partial birth abortion ban despite similar commerce clause concerns because the issue has been federalized by our courts and the moral imperitive [sic] to ban such an abhorent [sic] practice was so strong."

Despite our desire to advance the pro-life cause, the Constitution, as previously noted, doesn't simply establish perimeters on the power of the federal government when we dislike a particular bill. Rather, its boundaries are firm and unchangeable no matter how much we would like to make an exception "just this one time."

Certainly federal candidates should pledge to pursue Congressman Paul's Sanctity of Life Act of 2011 and/or a constitutional amendment overturning Roe, but they shouldn't seek to overturn an unconstitutional court decision by in turn using unconstitutional congressional power. The Constitution imposes road blocks on Congress which must be enforced regardless of personal desires. That is the hard task of the law.

HOW THE CONSTITUTION LOST AGAIN
(April 1, 2012)

"This was a train wreck for the Obama administration," CNN legal correspondent Jeffrey Toobin bemoaned after the U.S. Supreme Court heard oral arguments on the constitutionality of Obamacare's individual mandate. "This law looks like it's going to be struck down." While that may be so, the constitutional victory will be largely symbolic and may actually speed the rise of socialized medicine in America.

Since 1942 the Supreme Court has held that the federal government has the authority to regulate purely local intrastate, non-commercial activity that might have some aggregate affect on interstate commerce, and no one asked the Court to overturn this unconstitutional precedent. Instead, the opponents of Obamacare conceded that, under current precedent, Congress could socialize health care, they just went about it the wrong way.

Rather than challenge the Court's most egregious precedents, opponents of the individual mandate sought to explain why a case such as Wickard v. Filburn "that holds that a farmer has engaged in interstate commerce when he feeds his own grain to his own cows cannot be read to allow Congress to impose a duty on individuals to pay a fine if they do not take out health care for their own protection."

Their solution? That, unlike the Court's previous cases, "the mandate is not conditional upon anyone having taken an affirmative step...Roscoe Filburn was only subject to the Agricultural Adjustment Act because he chose to produce wheat for his dairy cows. The mandate, on the other hand, does not require a similar predicate. Someone else can be subject to the mandate even if they have done nothing at all."

Conceding that Wickard was correctly decided, Paul Clement, the attorney for the opponents of Obamacare, opened his argument before the Court by stating that the "mandate represents an unprecedented effort by Congress to compel individuals to enter commerce in order to better regulate commerce."

Taken with this argument, Justice Kennedy, widely assumed to be the swing vote, asked the government's attorney whether it could "create commerce in order to regulate it?" Minutes later he hinted that the individual mandate, by creating an "affirmative duty to go into commerce," was "unprecedented" and a "step beyond what our cases have allowed."

Rather than arguing over whether the Constitution gives Congress the power to pass Obamacare, opponents of the law argued over whether or not this or that Supreme Court opinion gave Congress the power to pass the individual mandate. Neither the justices nor the attorneys went back to first principles by analyzing the original public understanding of the Constitution.

As noted constitutional scholar Richard Epstein remarked last year, "What is so striking about these arguments [against Obamacare] is that none of them starts with the text of the Commerce Clause itself...How does anyone wrench Wickard v. Filburn out from a clause that says that 'Congress shall have power . . . To regulate commerce with foreign nations, among the several states, and with the Indian tribes.' It beats me how a provision that is drafted to allow Congress the important power to deal with transportation, communication, and the shipment of goods across state lines, can be expanded to let it regulate any activity that affects commerce, even if done in a purely local setting."

As Justice Thomas has previously warned, "holding that Congress may regulate activity that is neither interstate nor commerce under the Interstate Commerce Clause, the Court abandons any attempt to enforce the Constitution's limits on federal power...Federal power expands, but never contracts, with each new locution [by the Supreme Court]. The majority is not interpreting the Commerce Clause, but rewriting it."

Even if the Court strikes down the individual mandate, the majority will make no effort to limit or overturn its existing caselaw to return the federal government to some resemblance of one with limited, enumerated powers. So while constitutionalists may win the battle over the mandate, they will lose the war.

Instead, the argument made by opponents of Obamacare is simply one of timing. As the attorney for the government reasonably pointed out twice at oral arguments, "I think it's common ground between us and the Respondents that this is an interstate market in which everybody participates. And they agree that -- that Congress could impose the insurance requirement at the point of sale. And this is just a question of timing, and whether Congress's - whether the necessary and proper authority gives Congress, because of the particular features of this market, the ability to impose the -- the insurance, the need for insurance, the maintenance of insurance before you show up to get health care rather than at the moment you get up to show."

In pressing opponents of the individual mandate about this, Justice Sotomayor asked, "Do you accept your -the [Solicitor] General's position that you have conceded that Congress could say, if you're going to consume health services, you have to pay by way of insurance?" Without any hesitation, Paul Clement answered in the affirmative that "if you regulate the point of sale, you regulate commerce, that's within Congress's commerce power."

With this concession, challengers of Obamacare concede that, once an individual enters the market, they are subject to Congressional regulation. For example, instead of impermissibly requiring individuals to buy health insurance before they enter the health care market, they agree that Supreme Court precedent correctly allows Congress to require individuals to buy health insurance at the time they need health care.

Additionally, Supreme Court precedent gives Congress the authority to dictate the type and manner of health insurance plans existing participants in the health care market must purchase. Furthermore, the federal government could require existing health care participants to join a health club, eat vegetables, or get annual colonoscopies.

Remember IPAB? The Independent Payment Advisory Board created under Obamacare to control medical costs (i.e., a death panel)? No one has challenged its dubious constitutionality on the grounds that Congress lacks the authority to ration health care costs. Rather, it is being challenged in court on the principle that Congress has no "constitutional power to delegate nearly unlimited legislative power to any federal executive branch agency." In short, the challengers concede that the federal government has the power but, as it is currently exercised, it violates the principle of separation of powers.

Similarly, legal challenges to Obama's contraception mandate under Obamacare are based on the First Amendment's protection of religious liberty rather than on Commerce Clause grounds. The challenges concede that the Supreme Court's unconstitutional precedent gives the federal government the authority to impose such a mandate; they only argue that, in this particular instance, it cannot be imposed on conscientious objectors.

By failing to relitigate existing Supreme Court precedent, challengers of the various provisions of Obamacare concede that the federal government has the power to pass the legislation, but argue only that it may have used the wrong method or violated a constitutional right.

Even if they win in court, therefore, it will do nothing to stop the implementation of socialized medicine in America by different means. In all likelihood, it will only serve to speed it up, with those already suggesting the creation of a single payer system by simply expanding Medicare for everyone.

Justice Kennedy already signaled his approval of such an approach at oral arguments when he pointed out that Congress already has an alternative to the individual mandate by using "the tax power to raise revenue and to just have a national health service, single payer...In the one sense, it can be argued that this is what the government is doing; it ought to be honest about the power that it's using and use the correct power."

The means may be different but the end will remain unchanged. Socialized medicine by any other name is still socialized medicine. In striking the individual mandate but failing to overturn, at least in part, some of its most unconstitutional precedent, the Supreme Court will have accomplished little to restore a federal government of limited, enumerated powers.

TRAYVON MARTIN—A FEDERAL HATE CRIME? (April 10, 2012)

In the aftermath of unrestrained liberal hysteria over the Trayvon Martin shooting in February, the U.S. Justice Department decided to open an investigation into the incident. Without so much as a thought about the constitutionality of such action, members of the party that allegedly stands for a federal government of limited, enumerated powers were quick to praise the federal investigation.

Republican presidential candidate Mitt Romney issued a statement that ‘there needs to be a thorough investigation that reassures the public that justice is carried out with impartiality and integrity.” Senate Minority Leader Mitch McConnell (R-Ky) told reporters that he’s “glad it’s being investigated.” Tea Party favorite and potential Republican Vice-Presidential nominee Rep. Allen West (R-Fla) called the shooting “an outrage” and that he had “signed a letter supporting a DOJ investigation.”

Sadly, not a single member of the GOP questioned the constitutionality of federal hate crime charges that could potentially be brought by the DOJ against the shooter, George Zimmerman. To date, there is no evidence that would prove beyond a reasonable doubt that Zimmerman unjustifiably shot and killed Martin because he was black.

Assuming, however, that such evidence existed, there is no constitutional provision that would allow Congress to make such a murder, no matter how heinous, a federal crime. Though we may like the desired result, the Constitution’s boundaries are firm and unchangeable no matter how much we would like to make an exception “just this one time." The Constitution is an equal opportunity prohibition of federal authority.

Current federal hate crime law punishes crimes committed "because of the actual or perceived religion, national origin, gender, sexual orientation, gender identity, or disability" of the victim.

Two separate Democratic Justice Departments have argued that the statute is constitutional under the Thirteenth Amendment, which reads that: "Neither slavery nor involuntary servitude, except as a punishment for crime whereof the party shall have been duly convicted, shall exist within the United States, or any place subject to their jurisdiction."

How is it that one can read the Thirteenth Amendment to prohibit criminal activity, though racial in nature, if it has nothing to do with "slavery or involuntary servitude?" One can't, unless you happen to be a justice on the Supreme Court. In the Civil Rights Cases of 1883, the Court held that "Congress has a right to enact all necessary and proper laws for the obliteration and prevention of slavery with all its badges and incidents."

Subsequent cases have taken the phrase "badges and incidents" and stretched it beyond any tenuous connection to slavery. In Griffin v. Breckenridge (1971), for instance, the Court held that "the varieties of private conduct that [Congress] may make criminally punishable or civilly remediable extend far beyond the actual imposition of slavery or involuntary servitude...Congress has the power under the Thirteenth Amendment rationally to determine what are the badges and the incidents of slavery."

These subsequent decisions have overlooked the fact that the Court, in the Civil Rights Cases of 1883, explicitly rejected this extension. After noting that the Thirteenth Amendment "has respect not to distinctions of race or class or color, but [only] to slavery," the Court concluded that "it would be running the slavery argument into the ground to make it apply to every act of [private] discrimination..Mere discriminations on account of race or color were not regarded as badges of slavery."

Proponents of federal hate crime legislation also argue for its constitutionality under the Supreme Court's unconstitutional Commerce Clause precedent. Indeed, the statute requires some nexus to interstate commerce in order for it to be applicable. But how could Martin's death, which took place within a single state, be connected with interstate commerce? Because it partly took place on a road (i.e., a "channel of interstate commerce") and the gun was likely manufactured out-of-state.

Seem far-fetched? Last month twelve individuals were charged under the statute for an Amish-on-Amish "hate crime" in Ohio. Their connection to interstate commerce? They traveled on roads to commit the crime, and the clippers used in the assault had been manufactured out-of-state. Originally understood, however, the Commerce Clause didn't even reach such activity as agriculture, production, or manufacturing, much less non-commercial intra-state road travel.

In the end, there is nothing in the Constitution that provides Congress with the power to criminalize hate crimes, and, rather than praising it, Republicans should have denounced the DOJ investigation of Zimmerman as an unconstitutional extension of federal power.

CONSTITUTIONAL GENOCIDE

(June 3, 2012)

Ron Paul, as some commentators have pointed out, is a pro-life fraud who played the abortion issue in hopes of winning social conservative voters in his bid to win the Republican nomination for president. Like all politicians, he whispered sweet nothings to the electorate while sweeping constitutional restraints under the rug. We should not, however, be applauding the sweet nothings but his return to constitutionalism now that the primary is over.

In the wake of recent undercover investigations showing women seeking abortions based on the gender of their unborn child, the House voted recently on the Prenatal Non-Discrimination Act of 2012. All but twenty Democrats voted against the legislation, while all Republicans, save for Congressman Paul and six others, voted for it.

Though not surprising, it is doubtful liberals would have taken the same position if abortions were performed because of race or the presence of the "gay gene." In contrast to those interest groups, however, the "women's rights movement" would rather protect a woman's "right to choose" than a woman's right to live.

Ron Paul, speaking on the House floor, explained the reasons for his vote: "I certainly share my colleagues' revulsion at the idea that someone would take an innocent unborn life because they prefer to have a child of a different gender. However,...Congress's jurisdiction is limited to those areas specified in the Constitution. Nowhere in that document is Congress given any authority to address abortion in any manner."

The bill itself claims constitutional authority under the Interstate Commerce Clause. However, since an abortion occurs entirely within a single state, that enumerated power is inapplicable even under the Supreme Court's "lax (but not-infinite) version of the interstate commerce power." Additionally, as Congressman Paul noted in 2003, such an interpretation would "inadvertently justify federal government intervention into every medical procedure through the gross distortion of the interstate commerce clause."

The bill also finds its justification in the provisions of the Thirteenth Amendment. That Amendment, however, only prohibits "slavery or involuntary servitude" and does not reach private acts of racial discrimination. Noticeably, the bill doesn't even attempt to explain of how murder, whether committed out of gender discrimination or not, constitutes slavery.

Finally, the bill justifies its ban on sex-selected abortions in the Fourteenth Amendment's grant of "power to enforce the prohibition on government action denying equal protection of the laws." The problem, however, is that it is implausible to argue that the absence of legislation can constitute state discrimination. A denial of equal protection only occurs when a state bans abortions performed because the child was a boy rather than a girl, or vice versa.

Failing that, others have argued that the bill is constitutional under the Fourteenth Amendment's guarantee of "life, liberty, or property." However, that provision simply requires that the law be followed before the government could execute a criminal, jail an individual, impose a fine, deprive a person of their estate, sentence them to exile, etc. The only right granted by this Clause was process—requiring the government to proceed according to the law of the land (i.e., constitutional and statutory provisions).

Yet others claim that the reference in the Declaration of Independence to the unalienable right to life mandates congressional action to ban all abortions. However, while "Declarational" law or natural law binds the conscience and can serve as the basis for new legislation or the civil disobedience of existing law, there is simply no evidence that the Founding Generation intended it as a grant of congressional power in the absence of constitutional authority.

There is a reason the Founders created a federal government of limited, enumerated powers—the long-term protection of man's unalienable rights to life, liberty, and property by decentralizing power. Though tempting, creating an exception just this one time out of "a desire to do good" will create a loophole that will "wield a power too great and terrible to imagine."

Like Sir Thomas More's response to his son-in-law in A Man for All Seasons, the constitutionalist denies the temptation to "cut a great road through the law to get after the Devil," knowing full well that, "when the last law was down, and the Devil turned 'round on" us, there would be no place to hide. As More concludes, "Yes, I'd give the Devil the benefit of the law, for my own safety's sake!"

The Constitution is an equal opportunity prohibition on federal power, leaving the solution, as always, at the state level.

WHO PROTECTS UNALIENABLE RIGHTS?

(June 18, 2012)

Does the protection of the unborn's unalienable right to life trump federalism? In the wake of Congressman Ron Paul's vote against the Prenatal Non-Discrimination Act of 2012, the pro-life community has questioned whether one could be both pro-life and a constitutionalist who maintains that the federal government is one of limited, enumerated powers. The answer to that question goes to the very heart of not only the purpose of government, but who is government.

Some, pointing to the acknowledgment in the Declaration of Independence that man is endowed by his Creator with an unalienable right to life, argue that, "since it is clearly spelled out in our Founding Document, it is the federal government's duty to protect that right, even if the states will not."

The problem, however, is that Congress lacks the enumerated constitutional authority to ban abortions. Again, some have argued that "protecting life falls under several of the purposes of government, spelled out in our Constitution: establish Justice, promote general welfare, secure the blessing of liberty." But these words, taken from the Constitution's preamble, have never been held to be a grant of federal power. Indeed, doing so would make the limited grants of power contained in the rest of the Constitution superfluous.

We are left, therefore, with the question of whether an unalienable right trumps constitutional restraints. In the absence of any constitutional authority, can the federal government exercise raw, unchecked power to, as the Declaration states, secure man's "unalienable rights [to] life, liberty and the pursuit of happiness"?

The only answer to that question consistent with natural law and human nature is an unflinching and absolute "no." Though we may desire to create an exception "just this one time" to preserve the life of the unborn, the history of human experience dictates that the exception will soon swallow up the rule.

For instance, House Democratic Leader Nancy Pelosi recently defended Obamacare on the grounds that it is "about life, liberty and the pursuit of happiness for the American people." Earlier in March, Pelosi declared that "it honored the vows of our founders: of life, a healthier life; liberty; the freedom to pursue our own happinesses."

Similarly, in defending New York City Mayor Bloomberg's ban on large soft drinks, Pastor Brian Carter proclaimed that the mayor was "fighting for your right to a longer and healthier life." Building on this "right," Bloomberg claimed that, "if government's purpose isn't to improve the health and longevity of its citizens, I don't know what its purpose is."

Secondly, if a right trumps constitutional process, what process remains? For instance, why couldn't the United Nations' Security Council pass a resolution making abortions illegal worldwide? In fact, one could argue that "if you believe life is a '[national] issue,' then you also must believe that a [nation] can decide to place into law that abortion is legal. That is not a pro-life stance."

Or, if rights trump process, why couldn't the president act without Congress by issuing an executive order banning all abortions? Or why couldn't the Supreme Court declare such unenumerated rights as a "right to die" grotesquely found in one's right to life, or a "right to capitalism" located in one's property rights, or the use of recreational drugs mandated by one's right to pursue happiness?

Likewise, why couldn't Congress overturn by simple statute, rather than constitutional amendment, Supreme Court decisions such as Roe v. Wade, which legalized the murder of the unborn, Kelo, which allowed the taking of property from A to give to B, or Dred Scott, which elevated slavery to a constitutional right?

Finally, and more fundamentally, government power—whether local, state, or federal—is illegitimate when used outside of its delegated limits. The defense of unalienable rights falls on We the People as individual sovereigns, and we in turn delegate that authority to civil government to serve as an impartial arbitrator Government is simply a social compact between We the People for the mutual defense of our unalienable rights from foreign and domestic threats.

Because all power corrupts, written constitutions memorializing this sacred pact between individual sovereigns on the degree and method of legitimate coercion were established. This written "consent of the governed"—the fundamental will of We the People—is only changeable though the amendment process.

All power, therefore, exercised outside of that delegated by We the People is an infringement on our natural right to individual sovereignty. This right to constitutional process cannot be trumped by other unalienable rights.

ELECTIVE MONARCHY

(September 25, 2012)

"The contest, for all ages, has been to rescue liberty from the grasp of executive power," warned Daniel Webster. "Through all this history of the contest for liberty, executive power has been regarded as a lion which must be caged," he continued, "it has been dreaded, uniformly, always dreaded, as the great source of its danger."

The fundamental lesson of history is that freedom and the protection of God-given unalienable rights are not the norm but the exception. Democracies are fleeting, and America is hardly immune to the historic reality that all republics have eventually dissolved into dictatorships.

In an attempt to postpone this inevitability, the Founding Generation established a written federal constitution with grants of limited, enumerated powers and counteracting checks and balances. In crafting the nature of the executive branch, the Constitution bestowed on the President twelve powers:

1. He may exercise a qualified veto.
2. He shall be Commander in Chief.
3. He may require the written opinion of cabinet members.
4. He shall have power to grant pardons.
5. He shall have power, by and with the advice and consent of two-thirds of the Senate, to make treaties.

6. He shall nominate, and by and with the advice and consent of the Senate, shall appoint ambassadors, judges, and all other officers of the United States, and shall have power to fill vacancies that may occur during a Senate recess.

7. He shall give Congress the state of the Union and recommend to their consideration such measures as he shall judge necessary and expedient.

8. He may, on extraordinary occasions, convene both Houses, or either of them.

9. He may, in case of disagreement between both Houses, with respect to the time of adjournment, adjourn them to such time as he shall think proper.

10. He shall receive ambassadors and other public ministers.

11. He shall take care that the laws be faithfully executed.

12. He shall commission all the officers of the United States.

That's it–only twelve grants of authority, none of which involve implementing one's own domestic policy agenda. The president's sole responsibility towards legislation was to "take care that the laws be faithfully executed." As drafter Roger Sherman noted, "the executive magistracy [w]as nothing more than an institution for carrying the will of the legislature into effect."

Joining him, James Wilson argued that the "only powers he considered strictly executive were those of executing laws." Echoing these sentiments, James Madison stated that the president should have "power to carry into effect the national laws...and to execute such other powers 'not legislative nor judiciary in their nature' as may from time to time be delegated by the national legislature."

In contrast, the modern (unconstitutional) welfare/administrative state produces presidents who craft legislation guised as executive orders and preside over legions of unaccountable, unchecked bureaucrats who churn out multitudes of new legislation each year. The fatal reality of social democracies is that there are far more lawmakers in the executive branch than there are in the legislative branch.

When this happens, the legislative branch becomes a mere nuisance, a road bump in the delivery of cradle to grave nannyism. This dysfunctional system leads to a chief executive who routinely promises that "If Congress won't act, I will."

When Washington promises to solve all our problems for us but fails to do anything but bicker, the electorate becomes ripe for a political savior. It is simple supply and demand—the electorate wants their Uncle Sugar Daddy, and a single executive is in a far better position to provide their fix than 535 squabbling congressmen.

When Washington becomes the center of all political power, the leadership the public expects cannot be provided by the petty benchwarmers in Congress. It can only be delivered by a single leader that leaves Congress castrated of all but an imaginary veto over the administrative state. The president acts, and Congress merely watches and complains.

Democracy lies at death's door when the election of a new autocrat, rather than congressional action, is the only realistic hope of altering executive branch lawmaking. Ironically, congressional attempts at utopia have, in the end, only weakened it vis-à-vis the president.

The only cure to this elective monarchy is to destroy the myth that Washington has any authority, moral or constitutional, to interfere with our lives. Unless the temple of statism in Washington is destroyed, it will eventually be subjected to the rule of a single high priest. And like too many religions, statism neither tolerates dissent nor rival ideologies.

4 CHECKS & BALANCES

PLAYING RECESS WITH THE CONSTITUTION

(April 5, 2010)

"It is disturbing that [the President] has exhibited a grandiose vision of executive power that leaves little room for public debate, the concerns of the minority party or the supervisory powers of the courts. But it is just plain baffling to watch him take the same regal attitude toward a Congress in which his party holds solid majorities in both houses."

That was the opinion of The New York Times in an editorial on January 9, 2006, when former President George W. Bush announced seventeen recess appointments while Congress was home for the Christmas holiday. Back then, the Times referred to recess appointments as a "constitutional gimmick" and an "end run," but they suddenly lost those principles when President Obama recently made fifteen recess appointments during Congress' Easter recess.

They aren't alone. In 2005, then-Senator Barack Obama called John Bolton, who President Bush appointed as his United Nations ambassador during a congressional recess, "damaged goods." Under the Bush White House, Senate Majority Leader Harry Reid would avoid taking full recesses in the Senate in order to prevent recess appointments, which he called "an end run around the Constitution," from being made.

Why the change of heart among Democrats? Obama attempted to justify his use of recess appointments by painting Republicans as obstructionists. "The United States Senate has the responsibility to approve or disapprove of my nominees. But if, in the interest of scoring political points, Republicans in the Senate refuse to exercise that responsibility, I must act in the interest of the American people..."

The reality, however, is that there was bipartisan opposition to several of Obama's nominees, including radical labor lawyer Craig Becker who had just been rejected by the Senate in February on a 52-43 vote. Also, as Senator Grassley pointed out, the vetting process of several of these nominees —specifically Jeffrey Goldstein and Alan Bersin— hadn't even been completed yet.

The Constitution specifically requires Senate approval of a presidential nominee, with one exception: "The President shall have the power to fill up all vacancies that may happen during the recess of the Senate, by granting commissions which shall expire at the end of the next [congressional] session." (Article II, Section 2, Clause 3) (emphasis added). This exception was necessary to, as the Times noted, "keep the government running smoothly in times when travelers and mail moved by horseback and Congress met part time."

The constitutional exception for recess appointments seems pretty straight forward—if a vacancy occurs during a congressional recess, the president could appoint a replacement without Senate confirmation. This does not, however, give the president the power to fill a vacancy if the office became vacant while Congress was in session. Nor does it give the president the authority to fill a vacancy that occurred while Congress was in recess but has since reconvened.

In the hands of the modern president, however, the exception to the Senate confirmation process has become the rule. Rather than only filling those "vacancies that may happen during the recess of the Senate," presidents over the past century have claimed the authority to fill any and all vacancies, regardless of when they occurred, so long as the Senate is in recess.

The New York Times and Senator Reid were right to call such an interpretation a "constitutional gimmick" and an "end run around the constitution." By claiming the power to make a recess appointment for any office so long as he waits until a recess to do so, the President transforms the Senate confirmation process from a constitutional mandate to simply an option that he can chose or reject at whim.

This power grab makes a mockery of constitutional restraints on presidential authority and should be denounced if any president, regardless of party, claims it.

SIGNING AWAY THE CONSTITUTION?

(August 25, 2010)

Can the federal government exceed its constitutional limitations simply by making a treaty that gives it that power? This question, which has been debated since the Constitution's ratification, has taken on a greater urgency over fears that the Senate may yet try to ratify the U.N. Convention on the Rights of the Child (UNCRC) this year before a new Senate takes office in January.

The UNCRC has been signed by every single country in the United Nations except for the United States and Somalia. President Clinton signed it in 1995 but never presented it to the Senate due to opposition from conservatives who argued that the treaty violated the rights of parents by subjecting such prerogatives to "the best interest of the child." President Obama, citing our failure to ratify the treaty as embarrassing, has promised to send it to the Senate for ratification.

But no where in the Constitution does it give the federal government any power to regulate intimate family decisions. Of the limited, enumerated powers listed in that document, none of them give the federal government the authority to interfere with the parent-child relationship in any way. With the exception of the Fourteenth Amendment, Washington lacks the ability to enter into a human rights treaty establishing the civil, political, economic, and social rights of anyone, children or otherwise.

Proponents of the UNCRC and other similar treaties argue that the Constitution does not place any restrictions on the ability of the federal government to enter into a treaty. For instance, then-Secretary of State John Foster Dulles infamously stated in 1952 that: "Treaties, for example, can take powers away from Congress and give them to the President; they can take powers from the states and give them to the Federal Government, or to some international body and they can cut across the rights given the people by the Constitutional Bill of Rights."

Tragically, Secretary Dulles did not reach this conclusion out of a vacuum. Years before Justice Oliver Wendell Holmes, in Missouri v. Holland (1920), had upheld a treaty that regulated the hunting of migratory birds because, according to the Court, a treaty could provide Congress with the power to regulate an area that the Constitution otherwise denied it. The Court later affirmed this theory in United States v. Curtiss-Wright Export Corp. (1936).

The Supreme Court finally reversed direction in Reid v. Covert (1957) when it ruled that "no agreement with a foreign nation can confer power on Congress, or on any other branch of Government, which is free from the restraints of the Constitution... There is nothing in this language which intimates that treaties and laws enacted pursuant to them do not have to comply with provisions of the Constitution."

The cause for so much confusion over the issue is the language of the Constitution's Supremacy Clause in Article VI. The Clause proclaims that all "Laws of the United States which shall be made in Pursuance [of the Constitution...] shall be the supreme Law of the Land." Because treaties were declared to be the supreme law of the land only if they were made "under the Authority of the United States" rather than pursuant to the Constitution, many have argued throughout the years that the federal government's treaty making power was not bound by the Constitution.

But, as the Reid Court noted, "the reason treaties were not limited to those made in 'pursuance' of the Constitution was so that agreements made by the United States under the Articles of Confederation, including the important treaties which concluded the Revolutionary War, would remain in effect."

As those who drafted and ratified the Constitution made clear, the phrase "under the Authority of the United States" did not mean treaties could be made that violated the Constitution. At the Virginia ratifying convention, Governor Edmund Randolph responded to the fears of Patrick Henry and George Mason over the treaty making power by arguing that, "[b]eing creatures of that Constitution, can [the President and Senate] destroy it?"

George Nicholas agreed, contending that the federal government can "make no treaty which shall be repugnant to the spirit of the Constitution, or inconsistent with the delegated powers." Joining him, James Madison stated: "Here, the supremacy of a treaty is contrasted with the supremacy of the laws of the states. It cannot be otherwise supreme."

Thomas Jefferson argued that "I say the same as to the opinion of those who consider the grant of treatymaking to be boundless. If it is, then we have no Constitution." Elsewhere, Jefferson stated that "surely the President and Senate cannot do by treaty what the whole government is interdicted from doing in any way."

Alexander Hamilton, nationalist though he was, argued that the "only constitutional exception to the power of making treaties, is that it shall not change the Constitution..." Later, he wrote that "[a] treaty cannot be made which alters the Constitution of the country or which infringes any express exceptions to the power of the Constitution of the United States."

The power of the federal government to enter into treaties with other nations is limited to those specific, enumerated powers given to it by the Constitution. If that document does not grant the federal government the authority to regulate in a particular area, then it is powerless to accomplish such a feat by its treaty making power. The ability to ratify treaties simply does not grant the President and Senate the authority to rewrite and supersede the Constitution absent the amendment process.

CZARIST AMERICA

(September 22, 2010)

Last Friday, President Obama appointed Harvard law professor Elizabeth Warren to oversee the creation of the new Consumer Financial Protection Bureau (CFPB). The Bureau, part of the financial regulatory overhaul bill passed in July, is tasked with the responsibility to prevent abusive and deceptive practices in the mortgage and credit card industries.

Warren, the current chair of the congressional panel overseeing TARP and a rumored future Supreme Court nominee, will oversee an agency whose budget could be as large as $500 million. Treasury Secretary Timothy Geithner has set July 21, 2011, the one-year anniversary of the signing of the financial regulatory bill, as the target date for when the creation of the new agency would be completed.

Warren assumes her new "interim" position, which ostensibly ends next July 21st, without going through the Senate confirmation process. Such constitutional shenanigans had initially caused Chris Dodd (D-Conn), the current chair of the Senate banking committee, to threaten to defund the agency if Warren was appointed to lead it, even on an interim basis. After Obama made the appointment, however, Dodd issued a statement praising Warren as a "strong, qualified, and terrific watchdog."

Representatives Darrell Issa (R-CA), the ranking member of the House Committee on Oversight and Government Reform, and Spencer Bachus (R-AL), the ranking member of the House Financial Services Committee, showed more fortitude, demanding that the White House detail Warren's specific responsibilities and supervisory authority, which agency will pay her salary, and where she will file her financial disclosure statement.

In their letter to White House Counsel Robert Bauser, they wrote that Obama "is undermining Congressional oversight while giving her substantive authority over the CFPB. This is unprecedented...For the next ten months, it appears the CFPB will exist in a murky status that seems designed to obstruct Congressional and public scrutiny of its operations."

The White House hopes to avoid the "advice and consent" role of the Senate by naming Warren as "special advisor" to both the President and the Treasury Secretary. Better known in public parlance as czars, the first "special advisor" occurred when

Woodrow Wilson appointed financier Bernard Baruch to head the War Industries Board, a position dubbed industry czar.

Franklin Roosevelt created a dozen such czars during his presidency, and modern presidents since Richard Nixon have made increasing use of the position to place loyal, and at times controversial, supporters among career bureaucrats to ensure that the administration's policies are carried out.

With the recent addition of Warren and the Asian tarp czar, John Goss, the total number of current czars comes to 43. The large number of czars appointed by President Obama, particularly this early in his administration, led Senator McCain (R-AZ) to tweet last year that Barack Obama has more czars than the Romanovs, the Russian imperial family, ever did.

The problem is that Section 2 of Article 2 of the Constitution allows the president to appoint officers of the United States only with the advise and consent of the Senate. As the Department of Justice noted in 2007, a federal "officer" under this constitutional provision, commonly referred to as the Appointments Clause, is one who "is invested by legal authority with a portion of the sovereign powers of the federal Government."

The DOJ memo defined the term "sovereign powers" as the authority to bind "the Government or third parties for the benefit of the public, such as by administering, executing, or authoritatively interpreting laws."

Most presidents make the theoretically plausible, but practically dubious, claim that their czars do not satisfy this definition because they are merely advisers who lack any decision-making powers. Not so in the case of Warren's appointment to lead the creation of the new consumer protection agency.

As President Obama noted when he named her as the interim head of the CFPB, "she will help oversee all aspects of the bureau's creation, from staff recruitment to designing policy initiatives to future decisions about the agency. She will have direct access to me and to Secretary Geithner, and she will oversee a staff [of 30-40] at the Treasury Department that has already begun to work on this task."

This isn't the definition of a mere adviser offering her opinion to duly confirmed executive officials, but the job description of one who has the authority and discretion to make administrative and policy decisions on behalf of the federal government.

Unfortunately, the same can be said about a great many of the administration's unconfirmed czars. It is long past due for Congress to reassert its rightful role of "advise and consent" by demanding specific job information for each czar. If such information is withheld by the White House, or it turns out that the czar is in fact an "official" under the Appointments Clause, Congress should not hesitate to defund the agency.

It is time to restore checks and balances to the appointment process, and to place the selection of policymakers in the hands of duly-elected representatives of the people.

IOWA CONGRESSMEN DECLAR WAR ILLEGAL
(March 20, 2011)

A majority of Iowa's congressional delegation have argued that the president does not have the constitutional authority to use military force. Or at least they did in 2007, when the president's last name was Bush. Now that the president is one of their own, however, they have remained inexcusably silent, while their Republican colleagues have appeared divided over the scope of the president's powers.

Senator Harkin (D), along with twenty-nine of his Senate colleagues, wrote President Bush on November 1, 2007, that "no congressional authority exists for unilateral military action against Iran," and they warned that "offensive military action should not be taken against Iran without the express consent of Congress."

Democratic Congressmen Braley and Boswell co-sponsored House Joint Resolution 14, which stated that: "absent a national emergency created by an attack or imminent attack by Iran upon the United States, its territories or possessions or its Armed Forces, the President shall consult with Congress, and receive specific authorization pursuant to law from Congress, prior to initiating military force against Iran."

The two congressmen also co-sponsored House Joint Resolution 33, which similarly provided that "seeking congressional authority prior to taking military action against Iran is not discretionary, but is a legal and constitutional requirement." Citing historical precedent, the resolution stated that "initiating military action against Iran without congressional approval does not fall within the President's `Commander-in-Chief' powers under the Constitution."

In 2007, Boswell co-sponsored, and Congressman Loebsack (D) voted in favor of, Articles of Impeachment against Vice President Cheney for, among other things, threatening unauthorized military action against Iran. All four Democrats have declined efforts by The Iowa Republican (TIR) to learn why they were strident constitutionalists under the Bush Administration, but have yet to utter a denunciation of Obama's use of military force against Libya.

Republican Congressman King has also declined comment to TIR, but, appearing on Mickelson in the Morning on WHO Radio Wednesday, he stated that congressional authorization would only be needed if the mission became "extended in scope" or there were "boots on the ground." When pressed by Mickelson, however, he said that he would have to review the War Powers Act and may need to rethink his comments.

Through spokesmen, both Senator Grassley (R) and Congressman Latham (R) told TIR that the Act authorizes the President's actions, though they disagreed on the extent of the President's authority. Grassley's spokeswoman emailed TIR that if "the President intended to expand the scope beyond the mission of establishing and enforcing a no-fly zone,

Sen. Grassley would expect consultation with Congress and the need for congressional authorization would be based on the expanded mission."

In contrast, when asked whether Latham "believe[d] that the Act authorizes any and all force, including ground forces, without prior congressional authority," Latham's spokesman appeared to reply in the affirmative, noting that the "Act does not define the scope of 'introduction of U.S. forces.'"

On this question, the 2007 Democrats have articulated a position much closer to the Constitution than today's Republicans. As the War Powers Act notes, only Congress has the constitutional authority to declare war, while the President can only exercise military force "pursuant to (1) a declaration of war, (2) specific statutory authorization, or (3) a national emergency created by attack upon the United States, its territories or possessions, or its armed forces."

The President may also have the independent constitutional authority to launch strategic, even preemptive, defensive military actions, such as bombing Iran's nuclear facilities, drone attacks in Pakistan, the 1986 retaliatory strikes against Libya, or the 1989 Panama intervention after Noriega declared war on the U.S.

However, the present areal invasion of Libya and destruction of that country's air force, previously called an act of war by members of the Obama administration, clearly falls outside these limited inherit powers of the presidency and should be opposed by Congressmen of both parties.

SIGNING STATEMENT HYPOCRISY

(April 27, 2011)

The hue and cry of a constitutionally-conscientious Left was strangely silent as President Obama recently issued his 17th singing statement. Though negotiated by his Administration, Obama found several portions of the recently-passed budget bill for the remainder of Fiscal Year 2011 objectionable and, rather than vetoing it, issued a signing statement instead.

In particular, Obama objected to Section 2262, which defunded four of the President's czars that have not been confirmed by the Senate. In his signing statement, the President wrote that: "Legislative efforts that significantly impede the President's ability to exercise his supervisory and coordinating authorities or to obtain the views of the appropriate senior advisers violate the separation of powers by undermining the President's ability to exercise his constitutional responsibilities and take care that the laws be faithfully executed."

In what can only be described as a power grab, the President then concluded that "the executive branch will construe section 2262 not to abrogate these Presidential prerogatives." In other words, Obama will presumably continue to fund the positions, perhaps from his own stash, despite Congress' legitimate exercise of its constitutional authority over the purse strings.

But when asked in 2008 if, "when Congress offers you a bill, [will] you promise not to use presidential signing statements to get your way?," then-candidate Obama simply answered, "Yes." He continued: "We have a government designed by the Founders so that they'll be checks and balances...Congress' job is to pass legislation. The President can veto it or he can sign it. But what George Bush has been trying to do...is he's been saying that 'I can basically change what Congress has passed by attaching a letter'...That's not part of his power...I taught the Constitution for ten years. I believe in the Constitution and I will obey the Constitution of the United States. We're not going to use signing statements as a way to do an end run around Congress."

He gave a similar response here in Iowa. "I believe in checks and balances," Obama said. "I want an Administration that is upholding the Constitution, that is including Congress in decision-making...Over the last six years we've seen the Constitution of the United States treated as if it was a nuisance to be avoided as opposed to the foundation of our democracy."

Then-candidate Obama was far from alone in his criticism of presidential signing statements. The American Bar Association called them "contrary to the rule of law and our constitutional system of separation of powers" and urged presidential candidates in 2008 not to use them. Charlie Savage of the New York Times won a Pulitzer for reporting on President Bush's use of signing statements.

Here in Iowa, Democratic Senator Tom Harkin once argued that, "with his recent signing statement, once again [President Bush] has shown he views Congress as a nuisance rather than an equal branch of government under the Constitution."

Congressman Leonard Boswell (D) once voted in favor of impeaching President Bush because, "in violation of his constitutional oath to faithfully execute the office of President of the United States and, to the best of his ability, preserve, protect, and defend the Constitution of the United States, and in violation of his constitutional duty under article II, section 3 of the Constitution `to take care that the laws be faithfully executed', has used signing statements to claim the right to violate acts of Congress even as he signs them into law."

Congressman Dave Loebsack (D) co-sponsored the still-born Presidential Signing Statement Act of 2007, which stated that the "judicial use of presidential signing statements is inappropriate, because it in effect gives these statements the force of law...Presidential signing statements are not passed by both Houses of Congress..., so they are not the supreme law of the land."

Where are these constitutionally-conscientious liberals now?

5 CIVIL RIGHTS & LIBERTIES

DOES THE CONSTITUTION PROTECT SLANDER?

(March 10, 2010)

Do protestors have the constitutionally protected right to picket your fallen soldier's funeral and harass the proceedings? That is the question the Supreme Court will attempt to answer after it agreed to hear Snyder v. Phelps—a case where the jury awarded a $5 million verdict against a Kansas pastor who has made headlines by protesting the funerals of fallen service members.

Four years ago, Marine Lance Corporal Matthew A. Snyder was killed while serving in Iraq and his family planned for a private funeral at their church. Rev. Fred W. Phelps, Sr., the pastor of Westboro Baptist Church in Topeka, Kansas, and six of his family members decided to stage a protest at the funeral.

The Westboro Baptist Church, which publishes the website www.godhatesfags.com, believes that God hates America because of the prevalence and tolerance of homosexuality, particularly in the military. During this particular funeral protest, they carried signs stating "God Hates the USA," "America is doomed," "Semper fi fags," and "Thank God for dead soldiers."

The father of the fallen marine, Albert Snyder, sued the protestors for, among other things, intentional infliction of emotional distress. The jury awarded Snyder $5 million in damages, a verdict which was later overturned by the Fourth Circuit Court of Appeals on the grounds that the protesters' speech was protected by the First Amendment.

The First Amendment, however, provides that, "Congress shall make no law...abridging the freedom of speech" (emphasis added). But there is no federal, state, or local law at issue in this case. No one is arguing that the government tried to suppress Rev. Phelp's speech in anyway.

This suit is entirely private in nature. It involved the offensive remarks made by one private individual against another private individual at a private event. In a type of personal injury suit, the aggrieved party sued the harasser in court for emotional damages.

How, then, does the First Amendment apply to this case at all? In cases such as New York Times v. Sullivan and Shelley v. Kraumer, the Supreme Court attempted to justify the First Amendment's reach into private suits by relying on the tenuous argument that, because the power of the state is used to enforce the verdict (i.e., through the court system), the government is in fact suppressing the speech at issue.

In essence, the Court reasons that, since the court system coercively transfers money from A to B because of A's speech, that it becomes a government restriction on speech. It is an ingenious but dangerous argument that brings every single court action under the Constitution's orbit. So long as there is a plausible political or social commentary behind one's actions, he is now immune from liability.

If this were the case, a minority resident would have no recourse against his prejudice neighbors if they decided to demonstrate outside his property every night, day after day. Or a host could not evict a rowdy house guest who was becoming verbally abusive if that guest was doing so as a political commentary. And suits for slander and libel would be impossible.

And taking the Court's precedent to its logical conclusion, no one could sue for monetary damages because, if awarded, the court would be depriving the defendant of private property without just compensation in violation of the 5th Amendment.

And no marriage could be dissolved because the Contract Clause prohibits states from breaking contracts.

Since these results were clearly not intended by the Constitution, the Court should use this case to overrule its past precedents and affirm that the mere application of neutral principles to enforce private suits does not constitute government action. The Constitution was intended to only govern public behavior, not private.

WICCAN ALTARS IN SCHOOL?

(March 16, 2010)

Can a student build a Wiccan altar in a school shop class? Should shop class be a religion-free zone? Must a teacher be forced to tolerate a religion he does not agree with and finds offensive? Where do the rights of a student begin and the teacher's end, and those of the other students?

These are questions that students, parents, and teachers at Guthrie Center are wrestling with after a shop teacher was suspended for telling a student he couldn't build a Wiccan altar in class. Dale Halferty, who has taught industrial arts at Guthrie Center High School for three years, was placed on an unpaid five-day suspension for his actions.

That five-day suspension, however, has become an indefinite suspension as Halferty, citing his Christian beliefs, refuses to change his position. Halferty argues that the school district is violating his right to freely exercise his religious faith when it forces him to act against his conscience.

"Personally, I think its offensive to worship rocks and trees," Halferty said. "I am just trying to be moral. I don't know how we can profess to be Christians and let this go on." Apparently, a number of students agree with him, with nearly 70 signing a petition stating that they did not want witchcraft practiced at the school.

Halferty, however, overstates his crises of conscience. He is not being asked to choose between teaching something that conflicts with his moral beliefs and his job. Christian teachers, such as biology teachers who have to teach evolution or history teachers who can't talk about the role of Christianity in our country's founding, have a much more difficult test of faith.

But Halferty simply opened up his classroom for students to build projects that they wanted to do. His case is no different than a speech teacher who would let students pick topics for a class speech but, when one of them started discussing famous people who shared his religious beliefs, the teacher stops him because he finds the religion offensive. Just as the speech teacher isn't teaching anything about the student's religion, so Halferty isn't teaching anything about Wicca by allowing the student to build an altar.

Secondly, as a teacher, your freedom of religion ends when it causes you to single out and condemn a student for his religious beliefs. While Wicca, a religion which worships nature, practices magic, and believes in a female deity, may be offensive, the student cannot be discriminated against based on his religion, no matter how many other students, teachers, or parents may find the religion offensive.

While a majority may support Halferty's actions, or that of the hypothetical speech teacher described above, the majority should keep in mind that what is good for the goose is good for the gander. Pretending for the moment that such religious discrimination is constitutional, the time may come when the majority is Muslim or Hindu or Wiccan. Would we be so eager to endorse religious discrimination then, after we have lost our majority?

Finally, while it is unlawful for a teacher allow some religions in the classroom and censor others, it is completely permissible for him to limit student choices by telling them that they cannot build any religious objects in shop class or discuss any religious subjects in a speech. And this total ban appears to be what Halferty has actually done in his classroom.

According to Halferty, he previously told another student that he couldn't build a cross in the shop class, citing the separation of church and state. Though Halfety is wrong in interpreting the 1st Amendment to require a ban on religious subjects, it is perfectly constitutional for teachers to impose such a ban in order to maintain classroom civility.

If Halferty is in fact banning all religious projects in his class and not just Wiccan altars, the suspension should be lifted and he should be allowed to return to the classroom immediately, with an apology and back pay by the district.

THE UNWORKABLE WALL OF SEPARATION

(April 15, 2010)

Recently, U.S. District Judge Barb Crabb ruled that the National Day of Prayer was unconstitutional because it violated the separation of church and state which, she believed, was mandated by the Establishment Clause of the First Amendment. The ruling received little attention by the Obama Administration, which remained uncertain as to whether it would pursue an appeal.

The National Day of Prayer was first established in 1952, and the statute presently reads: "The President shall issue each year a proclamation designating the first Thursday in May as a National Day of Prayer on which the people of the United States may turn to God in prayer and meditation at churches, in groups, and as individuals."

It is this simple statement that Judge Crabb found to be constitutionally indefensible. In her ruling, she wrote that, "[i]n my view of the case law, government involvement in prayer may be consistent with the establishment clause when the government's conduct serves a significant secular purpose and is not a 'call for religious action on the part of citizens.'"

She determined that the National Day of Prayer failed that test, finding that it went "beyond mere 'acknowledgment' of religion because its sole purpose is to encourage all citizens to engage in prayer, an inherently religious exercise that serves no secular function in this context."

She concluded that, "the government has taken sides on a matter that must be left to individual conscience....[R]ecognizing the importance of prayer to many people does not mean that the government may enact a statute in support of it, any more than the government may encourage citizens to fast during the month of Ramadan, attend a synagogue, purify themselves in a sweat lodge or practice rune magic."

Judge Crabb's ruling is only the latest example of the state of confusion that exists in the 1st Amendment's religion case law, particularly in the area of ceremonial deism. For instance, the Supreme Court has upheld the use of the motto "In God We Trust" on our nation's currency but, conversely, has held that the display of the Ten Commandments in a courtroom is unconstitutional.

The Supreme Court has held that manger scenes may be constitutional, but only if surrounded by a Christmas Tree, menorah, and Rudolph. It has held that prayer before the opening of a legislative body is constitutional, but lower courts have found some prayers to violate the 1st Amendment. The Supreme Court hasn't addressed the constitutionality of the Pledge of Allegiance yet, but in 2002 the 9th

Circuit found that it ran afoul the great wall of separation of church and state.

This condition of uncertain confusion in our nation's church-state case law rests on a profound misunderstanding of the Religion Clauses of the 1st Amendment, with the Supreme Court itself noting that, "[w]hile the two Clauses express complimentary values, they often exert conflicting pressures."

The problem lies in the fact that the courts have read into the Constitution two religion clauses when there is in fact only one—"Congress shall make no law respecting an establishment of religion, or prohibiting the free exercise thereof."

The Religion Clause was intended to protect a freedom—religious liberty—from the coercive power of government. The goal was not to simply prohibit a state church or the prosecution of a church by the state, but to prohibit all religious discrimination that can occur between these two sides of the same coin.

The only way to consistently protect all aspects of religious liberty is to read it as one unified clause prohibiting religious discrimination by the government. Such discrimination occurs in three primary forms—governmental denial of equal protection based on religion, government interference with a religious organizations beliefs and practices, or government coerced adherence to a particular religious faith.

Symbolic references to religion—National Day of Prayer, Ten Commandments, manger scenes, etc. —do not fall into any of these categories of government discrimination. Though generic endorsements may, as Justice O'Connor has noted, send "a message to non-adherents that they are outsiders," these "non-adherents" are not denied the equal protection of the laws because they fail to conform.

Nor does ceremonial deism present the threat of government interference with a church or organization's religious tenants and customs. Neither can symbolic references constitute coercion because they cannot reasonably and tangibly lead to government indoctrination and proselyzation.

It is time for the courts to replace their unworkable and conflicting religion jurisprudence with one that makes sense—that the Religion Clause is only violated by government religious discrimination.

TEAR DOWN THIS WALL OF SEPARATION

(April 21, 2010)

The Supreme Court made Jefferson's now infamous commentary of the First Amendment the foundation of its Establishment Clause jurisprudence when it declared in Everson v. Board of Education (1947) that the First Amendment "was intended to erect 'a wall of separation between church and State'...[that] must be kept high and impregnable. We could not approve the slightest breach."

For over sixty years now, this "wall of separation" has more often been used to advance religious discrimination by the government than as a means to prevent it. As then-Justice William Rehnquist noted in dissent in Thomas v. Review Bd. of Indiana, this "wall" has led to a tension between the Establishment Clause and the Free Exercise Clause, a tension which "was unknown at the time of the framing and adoption of the First Amendment."

This tension lies in a profound misunderstanding of the First Amendment—the courts have read into the Constitution two religion clauses when there is in fact only one: "Congress shall make no law respecting an establishment of religion, or prohibiting the free exercise thereof."

The Religion Clause was intended to protect a freedom—religious liberty—from the coercive power of government. The goal was not to simply prohibit a state church or the prosecution of a church by the state, but to prohibit all religious discrimination that can occur between these two sides of the same coin.

The only way to consistently protect all aspects of religious liberty is to read it as one unified clause prohibiting religious discrimination by the government. Such discrimination can occur in three primary forms: governmental denial of equal protection based on religion, government interference with a religious organization's beliefs and practices, or coerced adherence by the government to a particular religious faith.

Recently the Supreme Court heard oral arguments in a case in which the Christian Legal Society (CLS), which was denied official recognition as a student organization by Hastings College of Law because it refused to allow those who did not share its tenets to be members.

An officially recognized student organization at Hastings would have access to a number of privilege but, in order to enjoy them, a student group had to abide by the law school's non-discrimination policy.

The Christian Legal Society refused to change its bylaws to conform with the policy and sued in federal court. In a ruling, which was later upheld by the 9th Circuit without comment, the trial judge ruled that the non-discrimination policy did not violate the First Amendment.

Lost in the ruling, as happens too often in religion cases, is any discussion of the Religion Clause. But an essential component of religious liberty is the idea of institutional autonomy. As the Supreme Court itself has noted in Roberts v. United States Jaycees (2000), "[a]n individual's freedom...to worship...could not be vigorously protected from interference by the State unless a correlative freedom to engage in group effort towards those ends were not also guaranteed."

Religious institutional autonomy is violated when the government forces the organization to accept as members those who do not share its faith. To quote the Roberts Court again, "there can be no clearer example of an intrusion into the internal structure or affairs of an association than a regulation that forces the group to accept members it does not desire."

Hastings College of Law did exactly that, however, when it required CLS, as a condition to equal access of benefits enjoyed by other organizations, to allow individuals who do not share its beliefs to become members and serve as its officers.

This conduct falls in the intersection of two of the categories of religious discrimination described earlier—the denial of equal protection and the interference with the beliefs and practices (institutional autonomy) of a religious organization. If the decision is upheld, it will have far-reaching and dangerous consequences for churches, religious schools, and other non-for-profits seeking equal access in the public arena.

It is past time for the courts to replace their unworkable and conflicting religion jurisprudence with one that makes sense—that the Religion Clause is only violated by government religious discrimination.

ANONYMOUS SPEECH FOR PRO-FAMILY ACTIVISTS? (April 29, 2010)

On Thursday, the Supreme Court heard oral arguments on whether gay marriage activists can use a state's freedom of information act to compel disclosure of the names and addresses of those who signed a petition to overturn the state's domestic partnership law.

The state of Washington allows voters to veto acts of the legislature at the ballot box if they obtain a sufficient number of signatures to place the question before the voters. Using this process, a pro-family group called Protect Marriage Washington (PMW) collected 122,000 signatures to force a statewide vote on whether Washington's new domestic partnership law should be repealed.

In order to prevent a vote on the question, gay marriage activists attempted to have the courts throw the referendum off the ballot. That effort failed, and the veto referendum went before the voters last November, where it was rejected 53-47 percent.

Gay rights groups such as KnowThyNeighbor.org and WhoSigned.org also sought release of the signed petition forms that had triggered the referendum process. When the Washington Secretary of State's office announced that it would grant the freedom of information act request, PMW filed suit in federal court to stop the disclosure and won a temporary restraining order from the trial judge. On appeal, the injunction was overruled by the 9th Circuit but later reinstated by the Supreme Court when it agreed to hear the case.

A petition, unlike ordinary political speech, compels the government to do something (in this case, place an issue on the ballot) that it otherwise would not have done. During oral argument, Washington's Attorney General tried to use this distinction to argue that signing a petition is not speech protected under the 1st Amendment, but rather a part of the legislative process.

The problem with this argument is that all petitions force the government to place an issue or, more commonly, a political candidate's name on the ballot. To hold that all such advocacy is unprotected would have a chilling effect on the political process.

But why stop with petitions, since the act of voting itself compels the government to do something—whether it is repealing its laws or swearing in a new official? If signing a petition is not constitutionally protected free speech, than neither is the act of voting.

Rejecting Washington's argument, both the trial court and the 9th Circuit recognized, in keeping with Supreme Court case law, that signing a petition is political speech. They differed, however, in how much protection such political speech is entitled to when it is weighed against the public's "right to know."

PMW argued that the signers of the petition had a right to remain anonymous due to the real prospect of intimidation by gay marriage activists. Both KnowThyNeighbor.org and WhoSigned.org stated publicly that they intended to place the name and addresses of signers on the internet to encourage "uncomfortable conversations."

A local blogger had written that, if the leader of PMW "can do 'legal' things that harm OUR family, why can't we go to Arlington, WA to harm his family?" Boycotts were even threatened: "We shall boycott the businesses of EVERYONE who signs your odious, bigoted petition."

Several justices, in their questioning of counsel at oral argument, seemed to indicate a willingness to allow disclosure unless groups could show a "reasonable probability that [it would] subject them to threats, harassment, or reprisals."

But the Court should go even further and rule that individuals have the absolute right to anonymous speech under the First Amendment. The historic record illustrates the commonplace usage by our Founders of such pseudonyms as "Publius" and "Cato." They understood and cherished the important role of anonymous speech in our public debates and would not have approved placing the burden on a speaker to preserve his anonymity.

The right to anonymity is essential to the preservation of political speech, and the Court should take this opportunity to affirm its sanctity.

THE HOAX OF BIRTHRIGHT CITIZENSHIP

(May 5, 2010)

Playing the American jackpot—winning citizenship for your children simply by ensuring that they are born in the United States—not only encourages millions to enter this country illegally, but has spawned an entire industry that arranges for tourist visas for pregnant women so they clan fly to our country to give birth to an American citizen.

Many argue that citizenship based simply on being born in the United States is enshrined in the first sentence of the 14th Amendment, which reads: "All persons born or naturalized in the United States, and subject to the jurisdiction thereof, are citizens of the United States and of the State wherein they reside."

Some commentators have recently argued that those who drafted the 14th Amendment never intended to provide birthright citizenship to the children of those who are in this country illegally.

They contend that the phrase "subject to the jurisdiction thereof" excludes those who are citizens of another country.

They note that Senator Lyman Trumbull, a principal author of the Amendment, argued that this phrase meant subject to the complete jurisdiction of the United States, "[n]ot owing allegiance to anybody else." Senator Jacob Howard, another principal drafter, stated that the phrase means a full and complete jurisdiction, the same "in extent and quality as applies to every citizen of the United States now."

Others argue that the broad language of the Amendment was intended, with few exceptions, to grant birthright citizenship to everyone born in the United States. Senator Trumbull, for instance, also stated that "birth entitles a person to citizenship, that every free-born person in this land, is, by virtue of being born here, a citizen of the United States."

Senator Howard voiced his agreement, arguing that every person born within the limits of the United States "is by virtue of natural law and national law a citizen of the United States." During Congressional debates, another senator, Justin Morrill, asked, "As a matter of law, does anybody deny here or anywhere that the native born is a citizen, and a citizen by birth alone?"

This search for what limits, if any, those who ratified the Amendment intended to place on birthright citizenship is inconclusive. The reason, however, is not because its ratifiers intended to extend birthright citizenship to the children of illegal immigrants, but because it wasn't an issue in the late 1860s when the Amendment was drafted, debated, and ratified.

In fact, there was no such thing as an illegal immigrant until Congress start to pass laws restricting immigration in the 1880's. The historical record will never reveal whether those who placed birthright citizenship in the Constitution intended to extend it to children of illegal immigrants because such a concept was, pun intended, foreign to them.

The purpose of this clause in the 14th Amendment was to reverse the Supreme Court's decision in Dred Scott v. Sanford (1856), which held that blacks were not and could not be citizens of the United States. It sought to guarantee blacks national citizenship and entitle them to the same rights as everyone else.

There is nothing in the historic record to warrant the jump from guaranteeing birthright citizenship for the recently freed black man to enshrining it for the progeny of illegal immigrants.

The Constitution cannot be read to allow a parent, by giving birth in this country, to grant her child a citizenship that Congress has lawfully denied.

As the Court itself noted in Elk v. Wilkins (1884), "no one can become a citizen of a nation without its consent," and there can be no more forceful denial of consent than to make one's presence in the country illegal. It defies credibility to read the Constitution to allow Congress the authority to deny entrance to an individual and his unborn children but, once the feat is accomplished, the newborn offspring must be made citizens.

A child born to illegal immigrants in this country is just as unlawfully present in this country as his parents are, and granting that child birthright citizenship makes a mockery of Congress' power to regulate immigration. There is nothing in the historic record to show that those who ratified the 14th Amendment ever intended such a ludicrous proposition.

MIRANDIZING TERRORISTS?

(May 6, 2010)

The recent botched Time's Square bombing and subsequent arrest of the would-be-bomber Faisal Shahzad as he was about to leave the country has once again renewed the debate over what rights, if any, suspected terrorists are entitled to. Are they entitled to Miranda warnings? Do they have a right to an attorney? Should they be tried in civilian courts or military tribunals?

In this case, the Justice Department opted to initially interrogate Shahzad without reading him his Miranda warnings under the public safety exception to the Miranda requirement. It was only after they determined that there were no other "ticking bombs" that the FBI read Shahzad his Miranda rights. Shahzad, who will be tried in civilian courts, opted to continue cooperating with investigators.

Like the Christmas Day bomber before him, the Justice Department's decision to Mirandize Shahzad and try him as a civilian prompted criticism by Republicans. Many urged the Obama administration to detain, at least initially, Shahzad as an enemy combatant in order to obtain as much information from him as possible without Mirandizing him.

Unlike the Christmas Day bomber, however, Shahzad is a United States citizen, had been residing in the country, and was detained before leaving the country for a crime committed while in the United States. As a result, the Supreme Court, under its current case law, would all but assuredly have ruled that Shahzad was entitled to Miranda warnings before his statements could be used against him in court.

Lost in the recent discussion over whether federal agents should be required to Mirandize terrorists, regardless of their citizenship, is any debate over whether Miranda itself is constitutional. When the decision came down in 1966, it was widely denounced as another example of liberal policymaking by the Warren Court that had no basis in the Constitution itself.

President Nixon successfully campaigned on the issue in 1968, vowing to nominate judges who would follow the Constitution rather than engage in freewheeling policy debates. The federal Omnibus Crime Control and Safe Streets Act of 1968 was enacted to specifically overrule the Miranda decision, though the Department of Justice never attempted to rely on it.

Sadly, the furor over the Court's ruling in Miranda has died down to a whimper, if that. Shortly after taking the bench, the late Chief Justice William Rehnquist argued in Michigan v. Tucker (1974) that he regarded the Miranda warnings as "procedural safeguards" that are "not themselves rights protected by the Constitution."

However, when the Supreme Court finally had the opportunity to overrule Miranda in 2000, Rehnquist wrote the majority opinion in Dickerson v. United States that upheld the warnings because they had become embedded in routine police practice. Only Justices Scalia and Thomas dissented, arguing that, as the Court itself has held throughout the years, bad precedent does not become good law simply by becoming old bad precedent.

Miranda, should not be considered settled constitutional law, and the question over whether terrorists are entitled to Miranda warnings can be simply solved by overruling the decision. As a matter of public policy, the decision, as the Miranda dissenters pointed out, will "negate all pressures, [will] reinforce the nervous or ignorant suspect, and ultimately [will] discourage any confessions at all. The aim in short is toward 'voluntariness' in a utopian sense."

As a matter of constitutional law, the dissenters noted that the new warnings have no "support in the history of the privilege [against self-incrimination] or in the language of the Fifth Amendment." The Fifth Amendment guarantees that no person "shall be compelled in any criminal case to be a witness against himself," which traditionally was understood to simply mean that no one could be forced to provide involuntary, incriminating testimony against himself in a criminal proceeding.

Miranda does not become "settled law" simply by being repeated ad nauseam on Law and Order. In overruling it, the Court can make it easier for law enforcement officers to interrogate suspected terrorists without worrying about the possible inadmissibility of any confessions obtained simply because they failed to read the warnings.

CAN WE USE RACIAL PROFILING TO STOP TERRORISTS?

(May 16, 2010)

Political correctness seems to have run amuck lately in Washington over who exactly the terrorists really are. In his recent testimony before the House Judiciary Committee, Attorney General Eric Holder had a hard time even admitting that radical Islam could have contributed towards the recent acts of terrorism—the Fort Hood Shooting, the unsuccessful Christmas Day bomber, and the failed Time's Square bomber—in this country.

In the aftermath of the Fort Hood massacre, both the Obama Administration and the mainstream media tried to paint Nidal Malik Hasan as mentally unstable rather than a devout Muslim.

New York City Mayor Bloomberg, commenting on the possible identity of the would-be Time's Square bomber before his eventual arrest, stated that it was likely "a mentally deranged person or somebody with a political agenda that doesn't like the health-care bill or something."

These remarks seem absurd given the nature of the war on terror we are currently engaged in; a conflict begun by radical Muslims in which most, if not all, of those who have attacked us at home and abroad are Muslim Arabs.

But what role, if any, can race and religion play in the efforts of law enforcement? If we are supposed to be a color-blind society, how can we countenance racial or religious profiling by our government?

How can those of us who oppose affirmative action programs as a violation of equal protection also support the use of race by law enforcement officers? It has been argued, "[w]e conservatives can't have it both ways: either we're for race-neutral justice or we're not. We can't be against using race when it helps minorities but for it when it harms them — at least not without legitimate criticism as to our motives."

However, unlike affirmative action, the Supreme Court has traditionally held that there is only one valid exception to race-neutral policies—when national security demands it. As the Court put it in Korematsu v. United States (1944), "[p]ressing public necessity may sometimes justify the existence of [racial discrimination], racial antagonism never can."

The federal government had, in the months after the Japanese attack at Pearl Harbor, temporarily excluded Korematsu and others of Japanese descent from portions of the West Coast out of fear of espionage and sabotage. The Court ruled that this was constitutional "because we are at war with the Japanese Empire [and] because the properly constituted military authorities feared an invasion of our West Coast and felt constrained to take proper security measures."

Today we are at war not with the Japanese Empire, but with radical Muslims from the Middle East. This war, unfortunately, is not easily defined, has no obvious battle ground, and has an indefinite duration. Because of the sporadic nature of the war on terror, the government would not be justified in using the expansive use of race that was upheld in Korematsu.

The ongoing threat to national security posed by terrorists, however, would justify the limited use of race by law enforcement. A country cannot effectively fight and win a war if it must pretend that it doesn't know who its enemy is. If Britain had to pretend that the IRA was not Irish, or Israel that the PLO was not Arab, many innocent civilians would have perished from the subsequent inability of those governments to foil terrorist attacks.

We know who our enemy is, and we know most of them are from the Middle East and must find a way to enter our country, legally or otherwise, to commit terrorist attacks on our soil. Therefore, border and customs agents must be able to use race as one of several factors (example—race plus mildly suspicious behavior) when determining possible threats.

Likewise, we know that terrorists have an insatiable appetite for airplanes, and therefore those tasked with airline security are justified in using race as one of several factors when looking for possible suspects. The same could be said for officers patrolling the streets of Manhattan, which has proven to be a repeated target for terrorists.

This does not apply to local law enforcement officers, or even to federal agents generally. Instead, it only applies to those officers on "the front lines" of the battle against terrorism in our country. This limited and judicious use of race as one of several factors by "front line" officers is not only constitutional, but essential to our country's national security.

JUDGING MORALITY

(May 22, 2010)

Recently, the U.S. Supreme Court held that a life sentence without the possibility of parole for a juvenile convicted of a crime other than homicide was unconstitutional. In Graham v. Florida (2010), the Court found that this sentence violated the 8th Amendment's prohibition on cruel and unusual punishment, though it acknowledged that such a sentence may not have been understood by the drafters of that Amendment as being unconstitutional.

Graham, a juvenile at the time, and two of his friends attempted to rob a barbeque restaurant in Jacksonville, Florida. The robbers eventually fled the scene without taking any money, but not before they assaulted the manager with a metal bar. Pursuant to a plea agreement, Graham pled guilty in exchange for probation.

Less than six months after telling the court that "this is my first and last time getting in trouble," Graham was involved in an armed home invasion in which they held the occupants at gun point while they ransacked the home looking for money.

Later that same evening, Graham was involved in another home invasion in which one of his accomplices was shot. After dropping his wounded friend off at the hospital, Graham led police on a high-speed chase until he crashed into a telephone pole. In later questioning by police, he confessed to having been involved in two or three other home invasions prior to that night.

The court revoked his probation and sentenced him to life in prison, finding that, "[g]iven your escalating pattern of criminal conduct, it is apparent to the Court that you have decided that this is the way you are going to live your life and that the only thing I can do now is to try and protect the community from your actions."

Since Florida does not have a parole system, Graham's only hope of release was by executive clemency...or judicial empathy. A majority of the Supreme Court, relying on its amorphous 8th Amendment standard of "evolving standards of decency," ruled that the sentence violated the Cruel and Unusual Punishment Clause because it denied juveniles "any chance to later demonstrate [their fitness] to rejoin society."

Justice Kennedy, writing for the Court, held that, though the 8th Amendment did not necessarily prohibit a life sentence for a juvenile, it required states to "give defendants like Graham some meaningful opportunity to obtain release based on demonstrated maturity and rehabilitation."

Justice Stevens, along with Justices Ginsburg and Sotomayor, sought to justify in their concurrence the Court's power to gauge the "evolving standards of decency" by arguing that: "Society changes. Knowledge accumulates. We learn, sometimes, from our mistakes. Punishments that did not seem cruel and unusual at one time may, in the light of reason and experience, be found cruel and unusual at a later time..."

While that may be true, this standardless standard gives judges little guidance as to when and how far society has changed. But that is entirely the point of this and all other liberal judicial maxims—they are dressed up in just enough constitutional trappings to appease at least some of the public, while also vague and fluid enough to allow the justices ample ability to indulge in their favorite policy decisions.

"Evolving standards of decency" is nothing more than the substitution of the Court's own judgment in place of the legislatures' as to when, "in the light of reason and experience," a criminal punishment should be changed or modified. And in doing so in this case, it rejected the judgment of Congress, the District of Columbia, and 37 states which had allowed life sentences for juveniles in certain non-homicide cases and replaced it with its own.

Some commentators have commended the Court's decision, calling it the "right thing." But a morally "right" decision does not make a constitutionally "right" decision. Because judges are not arbitrators of morality but of the law, they must not, as Alexander Hamilton noted in Federalist #78, "substitute their own pleasure to the constitutional intentions of the legislature."

Judges are tasked by the Constitution with interpreting that document as its language was originally understood, not to attempt the impossible task of measuring the moral pulse of the country. It is long overdue, therefore, for the Court to abandon once and for all its unconstitutional "evolving standard of decency test."

ARE ABORTION, GAY SEX, & GUN RIGHTS THE SAME?

(June 28, 2010)

On Monday, the U.S. Supreme Court held in McDonald v. Chicago (2010) that the individual right to own a gun for self-defense, protected by the 2nd Amendment, does in fact apply to state and local governments. In doing so, however, four of the Court's five originalist justices engaged in the same sort of judicial activism that have led other majorities at other times to find a right to privacy, abortion, and homosexual behavior.

In its ruling on Monday, the Court did not directly touch on the 2nd Amendment at all, an amendment it had expounded on in D.C. v. Heller (2008) when it held that individuals had a right to possess firearms. Rather, the Court wrestled with whether or not that right applied to state and local governments through the 14th Amendment, and, in doing so, it used the very same reasoning it has employed to discover rights to abortion and gay sex.

By its terms, the 2nd Amendment and the other Bill of Rights do not apply to the states but only to Congress. The first ten amendments were only intended to restrict the power of the federal government over the individual, and in fact begin with the words, "Congress shall make no law..." The Supreme Court affirmed this original understanding of the scope of the Bill of Rights in Barron v. Baltimore (1833).

But all that changed when, in the aftermath of the Civil War, the 14th Amendment ensured that the newly freed bondsmen were U.S. citizens and that no state could "make or enforce any law which shall abridge [their] privileges or immunities [as U.S.] citizens."

While the phrase "privileges and immunities" may mean nothing to modern readers, those at the time of the ratification of the 14th Amendment understood it to simply refer those rights and liberties expressly enumerated in the U.S. Constitution, particularly in the Bill of Rights.

That seems straightforward enough—the entire Bill of Rights now applies to the states as well as to Congress through what is now called the Privileges and Immunities Clause. Unfortunately, the Supreme Court has flatly refused to do so because it would cramp their activism. Instead, beginning in 1897, the Court has used another provision to selectively chose which provision in the Bill of Rights it believes should be binding on the states, and therein lies the problem.

Right after the Privileges and Immunities Clause, the 14th Amendment goes on to prohibit states from denying life, liberty, and property without the due process of the law. The Court, seizing on the word "liberty," has opted to make rights in the first ten amendments binding on the states if they deem those rights to be fundamental to ordered liberty.

The problem with this theory, called substantive due process, is two-fold. First, as Justice Thomas noted in his concurring opinion, is that "[a]ll of this is a legal fiction. The notion that a constitutional provision that guarantees only 'process' before a person is deprived of life, liberty, or property could define the substance of those rights strains credulity for even the most casual user of words."

In other words, what is now called the Due Process Clause only guarantees process, such as notice of a new law or regulation or the opportunity to be heard before a judge. In fact, it allows for "life, liberty, or property" to be taken from someone, so long as adequate procedures are in place.

Rather than giving this clause its plain meaning, the Court has taken upon itself to define the term "liberty" and to hold that a person can never be deprived of that liberty, even if adequate procedural safeguards are in place.

As Justice Thomas noted, this license the Court has given itself to define the term "liberty" is "a particularly dangerous [fiction]. The one theme that links the Court's substantive due process precedents together is their lack of a guiding principle to distinguish 'fundamental' rights that warrant protection from non-fundamental rights that do not."

The Court has used substantive due process to not only cherry pick which Bill of Rights it thinks are important enough to apply to state and local governments, but it has also used the opportunity provided in defining the term "liberty" to find such rights as the right to privacy, abortion, and homosexual marriage that are no where to be found in the text of the Constitution.

Unfortunately, four justices of the five-member majority in McDonald used substantive due process to determine that the 2nd Amendment right to own a gun was fundamental enough to be included in the term "liberty" in the 14th amendment. By doing so, they not only continued to give validity to a dangerous theory that allows judges to find new non-textual rights, but it leaves open the possibility that a future majority may decide that gun rights might not be that fundamental of a right after all.

While the Court could have easily put a stop to this fount of judicial activism by ruling that the entire Bill of Rights was protected by the Privileges and Immunities Clause rather than leave future courts the ability to define the extent of the term "liberty," a majority of the originalist justices on the Court failed to failed to take this opportunity to do so.

OPERATION CHAOS

(July 19, 2010)

Recently, Illinois Governor Pat Quinn used an amendatory veto to create an open primary system in his state. Currently, Illinois operates a closed primary system in which voters must first register with a particular political party. Once they have declared a political party, the poll worker will then provide them with a ballot listing the names of the candidates running to represent that party.

By preventing a Republican from voting for a Democrat, or an Independent for a Green Party candidate, the closed primary system ensures that the eventual party nominee is actually the person chosen by members of that party. The majority of states currently operate some form of the closed primary, including Iowa and Illinois.

Under Quinn's changes to Illinois law, voters would no longer be required to state which party they belong to, if any. Under the illusion that voters are scared away from closed primaries because they would have to declare a party, Quinn argued that "Illinois' not about professional politicians...We need to use a crowbar to open up the process and let people vote in a primary without disclosure of their party."

Presumably, Illinois would only become a partially open primary because voters would still be required to vote only for one party's slate of candidates up and down the ticket. This would prevent, for instance, voters from voting for Republican candidates for governor and Secretary of State and Democrats for Lt. Governor (who, in Illinois, is selected by voters rather than the gubernatorial candidate) and Attorney General.

California voters, however, refused to share such restraint when they recently passed Proposition 14, better known as the Top Two Candidate Open Primary Act. Under California's new primary regime, all voters, even Independents, will receive the exact same ballot listing every single candidate for office.

Candidates will be designated with their party of choice, if they desire to list a party at all.

Unlike Illinois, voters in California will not be required to vote a straight party ticket but can instead vote for whichever party they desire for each office listed. The two candidates who receive the most votes will then face each other in a run-off, regardless of party affiliation. It is entirely plausible, therefore, that two Democrats could face each other in November for the governor's mansion, or two Republicans would end up on the general election ballot for the same Congressional seat.

The changes Illinois and California have made to their primary systems are just the latest in a disturbing trend towards abridging the ability of people to associate together for the purpose of political speech and choosing their candidate as their spokesman. The U.S. Supreme Court has long recognized the First Amendment rights of political parties to "associate with the persons whom they choose and to refrain from associating with persons whom they reject."

As a part of this right of political speech and association, political parties have the right to choose and promote the "standard bearer who best represents the party's ideologies and preferences."

As Justice Scalia noted in a 2008 dissent, "The electorate's perception of a political party's beliefs is colored by its perception of those who support the party, and a party's defining act is the selection of a candidate and advocacy of that candidate's election by conferring upon him the party's endorsement."

But open primaries flagrantly deprive political parties of their constitutional right to ensure that only their members choose their standard bearer. Under open primary schemes, a candidate can pick which party he wants to be affiliated with (even if they don't want him because he is unrepresentative of their platform) and be made that party's spokesman by voters who are not members of that political party.

Open primaries will also all but ensure that minor political parties such as the Libertarian, Green, and Constitution Parties will not be represented on the general election ballot come November because, in most case, their candidates will be unable to finish among the top two candidates in the primaries. Without such access to the ballot box, the Federalist Party would never have given birth to the Whig Party, which in turn gave birth to the Republican Party.

The ability of like-minded individuals to join together to form a political party to select a standard bearer who, if elected, would work to implement their political ideology is a core right protected by the First Amendment. It is imperative that courts vigorously protect that right by striking down open primary laws such as those in Illinois and California.

TARGETED KILLINGS OF U.S. CITIZENS
(September 8, 2010)

As Americans pause this Saturday to mark the 9th anniversary of the 9/11 terrorists attacks, the American Civil Liberties Union (ACLU) and the Center for Constitutional Rights (CCR) recently filed a lawsuit challenging the government's policy of using drones to kill American al-Qaeda terrorists.

Both groups filed suit on behalf of the father of Anwar Al-Aulaqi, an Islamic cleric living in Yemen who is believed to have ties to the Fort Hood massacre, the foiled Christmas Day "underwear bomber," and the attempted Times Square bombing. It has been reported that Al-Aulaqi has been placed on the government's "kill lists," though the administration, naturally, is not discussing the issue publicly.

The groups argue that targeted strikes of U.S. citizens by military drones are prohibited by both international law and the U.S. Constitution. Vince

Warren, the Executive Director of CCR, stated in a press release that the "United States simply cannot execute people, including its own citizens, anywhere in the world based on its own say-so. The law prohibits the government from killing without trial or conviction other than in the face of an imminent threat that leaves no time for deliberation or due process."

The lawsuit is a publicity stunt in which the groups frame the debate as one over the execution without trial of an American citizen abroad by his own government. But they go even further in their complaint by arguing that international law prohibits all "targeted killing of individuals," whether U.S. citizens or not.

The larger issue for the ACLU and CCR is not so much the citizenship but rather the location of the person targeted. Unless the terrorist is in an actual zone of armed conflict, "targeted killing amounts to the imposition of a death sentence without charge, trial, or conviction."

Their goal, made explicit in their complaint, is to stop drone attacks on all terrorists, regardless of citizenship, "except in circumstances in which they present concrete, specific, and imminent threats to life or physical safety, and there are no means other than lethal force that could reasonably be employed to neutralize the threats."

Outside of press releases, the issue of whether the targeted terrorists are U.S. citizens or not doesn't matter to the ACLU and CCR, nor should it. A terrorist is no less a terrorist because he happens to be a U.S. citizen. His goal of destroying the American infidels by any means possible is indistinguishable from that of other terrorists, and our response should likewise be indistinguishable.

The war for terror is being waged by both Americans and non-Americans, and it would be irresponsible for us to attempt to distinguish among terrorists in the field based on their nationality. While captured American terrorists may be entitled to rights under the U.S. Constitution that are not applicable to foreign terrorists, U.S. citizens who are actively engaged in treason do not enjoy a constitutional right to be treated any less harshly than their fellow terrorists.

Nor does the Constitution or international law require that the United States, or any other country, stop the pursuit of terrorists simply because they are currently not engaged in pitched battle. Even liberal legal academic and current State Department legal advisor Harold Koh argues that individuals "who are part of such an armed group are belligerents and, therefore, lawful targets under international law."

The ACLU and CCR fail to understand, as the Left too often does, that terrorism is not a law enforcement act that can be handled by ordinary prosecutorial tools. Nor are terrorists only engaged in terrorism when they actually blow things up or find themselves in a shoot-out with U.S. forces. Those who are actively engaged in planning attacks, raising money, and recruiting new soldiers are no less terrorists simply because no bullets happen to be flying or bombs going off at that time.

There are factors, of course, that should be considered before a missile strike is ordered. As Koh has noted, the administration considers "the imminence of the threat, the sovereignty of the other states involved, and the willingness and ability of those states to suppress the threat" before a strike is ordered.

Additionally, the administration already notifies the bipartisan leadership of the congressional intelligence committees in advance of any drone attack. Furthermore, under congressional supervision, there should be sufficient reviews and checks built into the process of designating kill targets to ensure reliable intelligence.

In the end, the nationality and location of the terrorist do not make a terrorist, his actions do. And if he is actively engaged in waging war on the United States or its interests, our nation has the right to defend itself by taking the war to him and eliminating the threat.

PARENTAL RIGHTS?

(November 12, 2010)

The Iowa Supreme Court's decision legalizing same-sex marriage in Varnum v. Brien (2009) was hardly the first example of judicial activism by the Court, nor does it seem like it will be the last. The goal of the anti-retention campaign to oust those justices on the November ballot was, in part, to send a message that justices who strayed from the Constitution will be fired. It is less than two weeks from Election Day, but it doesn't appear that a majority of the justices learned that lesson.

On Friday, the Supreme Court released its decision in Hensler v. City of Davenport (2010), in which it struck down Davenport's "Parental Responsibility" ordinance passed in 1999. In order to "preserve the peace, safety, health and welfare of the citizens of Davenport, Iowa, and the city's visitors and guests," the ordinance required a "parent of a minor...to exercise reasonable control over said minor" or face, after repeat offenses, a monetary fine.

Anne Hensler was cited twice under this ordinance and filed suit in district court, arguing that it "violate[d] her substantive due process rights [under the 14th Amendment] by interfering with her fundamental right to parent." The 14th Amendment to the U.S. Constitution prohibits States from depriving anyone of "life, liberty, or property, without due process of law."

What is now known as the Due Process Clause simply requires that the law be followed before the government could execute a criminal, jail an individual, impose a fine, deprive a person of their estate, sentence them to exile, etc. The only right granted by this Clause was process—requiring the government to proceed according to the law of the land (i.e., constitutional and statutory provisions).

The Clause doesn't even require a certain level of process, leaving other constitutional provisions to protect fundamental criminal procedural rights such as a right to counsel, to an indictment, to a speedy and public trial, and against double jeopardy.

As Justice Hugo Black noted in his dissent in In Re Winship (1970), "'Due process of law' was originally used as a shorthand expression for governmental proceedings according to the 'law of the land' as it existed at the time of those proceedings." In short, the Clause was never intended to strike down a law for violating "due process", but rather to make sure the due process required by existing laws was followed.

Abandoning this straightforward meaning, modern courts have eagerly interpreted the Clause to require that "the government [cannot interfere] with 'rights implicit in the concept of ordered liberty.'" The difficulty is that, unmoored from its original meaning, judges are free to define what constitutes "liberty" and "process" as they see fit, and under the guise of this theory courts have created such novel unenumerated rights as privacy, abortion, and homosexual sodomy.

The problem with this theory, often called substantive due process, is, as Justice Clarence Thomas noted in his concurrence in McDonald v. Chicago (2010), that "The one theme that links the Court's substantive due process precedents together is their lack of a guiding principle to distinguish 'fundamental' rights that warrant protection from non-fundamental rights that do not."

Substantive due process allows a court, as Justice Black argued, to "free itself from the limits of a written Constitution and sets itself loose to declare any law unconstitutional that 'shocks its conscience,' deprives a person of 'fundamental fairness,' or violates the principles 'implicit in the concept of ordered liberty'...[S]uch an arrogation of unlimited authority by the judiciary cannot be supported by the language or the history of any provision of the Constitution."

Unfortunately, an unanimous Iowa Supreme Court engaged in exactly that kind of unprincipled activism in Hensler as it held that parents do have an unenumerated right to raise their children under the theory of substantive due process. As much as we may agree with this right and believe it should be protected by the Constitution, it simply is not provided for in the text of that document.

But having discovered this right, the Court ultimately concluded that the ordinance "only minimally impinges on a parent's fundamental right to direct the upbringing of his or her child" and therefore did not violate the 14th Amendment.

Instead, the Supreme Court struck down the ordinance for violating the Clause because it placed a presumption of wrongdoing on the parent that the Court determined was arbitrary and irrational. As explained earlier, however, the Clause doesn't prescribe a minimum procedural threshold, only that the existing constitutional and statutory procedures must be followed. The law was followed in this case, and the Court should have upheld Davenport's Parental Responsibility ordinance.

Despite a successful anti-retention campaign that ousted three of the Court's activist justices, the Court appears to be slow in understanding the message. The campaign was not a referendum on Bob Vander Plaats or even on marriage, but was over the proper role of the courts in our society. Though the people rejected judges who discovered policy and rights from the bench, the Iowa Supreme Court appears unwilling to relinquish its self-assigned role as societal shepherds.

CRUEL AND UNUSUAL

(November 17, 2010)

This past Monday night, Michael Richard Swanson shot and killed two convenience store clerks despite the fact that they had complied with his every demand. Swanson, a 17 year old teenager from Minnesota, had made his way to Iowa in a vehicle he stole from his mother and armed with weapons he apparently took after breaking into the family's cabin.

Facing two first-degree murder counts, Swanson appeared smirking and laughing as he was transported from the jail to the courthouse where the judge set his bond at $1 million cash only. When asked why he was laughing, Swanson simply replied, "Y'all are funny."

According to authorities, Swanson told them he had intentionally killed the women so they couldn't call 911 or later identify him. At least one of the murders, however, was caught on video, and police found the murder weapon and the stolen cash and cigarettes on Swanson when they later arrested him at a McDonalds.

These senseless, random, and clearly intentional murders have sparked anger and frustration that the death penalty does not exist in Iowa for cases exactly like this. Iowans have had a long and strange love-hate relationship with the death penalty. Capital punishment was provided for both before and after statehood until Governor Cyrus Carpenter signed a bill abolishing the penalty in 1872.

Given the inability to legally impose the death penalty, lynch mobs infamously took matters into their own hands in 1874, 1875, and 1877, prompting the Iowa General Assembly to reinstate the death penalty in 1878. Iowans again had a change of heart in 1965, when Governor Harold Hughes signed a bill that abolished capital punishment. A total of 41 people have been executed in Iowa at both the state and federal level.

Since then, numerous attempts have been made to reinstate the death penalty. Reinstatement bills made it out of either a legislative committee or an entire house of the Iowa General Assembly in 1970, 1975, 1976, 1993, 1995, 1997, and 1998. Governor Terry Branstad made capital punishment a major part of his 1990 gubernatorial campaign.

Though the issue has largely been ignored during the past decade, these recent murders, with Branstad once again in the governor's mansion, could provide the impetus to bring back the death penalty after 45 years. If passed, however, such a law would face a dubious future as its constitutionality would be decided by an Iowa Supreme Court on which four activist judges still sit.

A majority of the U.S. Supreme Court has consistently held that the death penalty, per se, does not violate the 8th Amendment's prohibition on cruel and unusual punishment, though the Supreme Court has held that it does so when applied to non-capital offenses, juveniles, and the mentally retarded.

The Iowa Constitution, however, contains its own guarantee against cruel and unusual punishment in Section 17 of Article I, and the Iowa Supreme Court has not hesitated in the past to interpret a provision of the state constitution differently than the U.S. Supreme Court's interpretation of the identical provision in the federal Constitution.

Despite the fact that both the U.S. and Iowa Constitutions specifically allow for capital punishment provided that due process of the law is followed, many activist judges share the belief that, because they find the penalty morally reprehensible, it also has to be unconstitutional.

In Furman v. Georgia (1972), for instance, a majority of the U.S. Supreme Court ruled that the death penalty could violate the Cruel and Unusual Punishment Clause, though they couldn't agree how. Justices William Brennan and Thurgood Marshall held that the death penalty was always unconstitutional, while others simply concluded that "the Eighth and Fourteenth Amendments cannot tolerate the infliction of a sentence of death under legal systems that permit this unique penalty to be so wantonly and so freakishly imposed."

As Justice Kennedy noted in his majority opinion in Roper v. Simmons (2005), it has become settled U.S. Supreme Court practice to refer to "'the evolving standards of decency that mark the progress of a maturing society' to determine which punishments are so disproportionate as to be cruel and unusual." Skewing any evolving standards but their own, these activist judges have bluntly declared that "the Constitution contemplates that in the end our own judgment will be brought to bear on the question of the acceptability of the death penalty under the Eighth Amendment."

Sadly, such an activist interpretation of the Cruel and Unusual Punishment Clause appears an ideal fit for an Iowa Supreme Court that recently ruled in Varnum v. Brien (2009) that the "Equal Protection Clause looks forward, serving to invalidate practices that were widespread at the time of its ratification and that were expected to endure.."

Any attempt to reinstate the death penalty, therefore, will fail until real judicial reform is established that exposes and prevents activists from assuming the bench in the first place. Until then, all our striving is in vain.

EQUAL VOTING RIGHTS?

(December 12, 2010)

Several Iowans recently filed suit in federal court, claiming that the state's current judicial selection process is unconstitutional and requesting the court for an injunction prohibiting the state nominating commission from selecting finalists for the three pending vacancies on the Iowa Supreme Court. Though doubtless well-intentioned, the suit asks the court to engage in the same type of judicial activism that Iowans rejected when they ousted the three Supreme Court justices.

In its complaint, the lawsuit argues that:

> Invariably, one of the three nominees selected by the Commission will become a justice or judge in Iowa, so that the Commission determines the composition of the judiciary in Iowa. Despite having this significant power and function, seven of the fifteen members of the Commission are elected exclusively by the members of the bar of Iowa. This restricted election denies the citizens of

> Iowa the right to vote and the right to participate equally in the selection of justices and judges in Iowa. (emphasis added)

Though similar lawsuits in Alaska and Kansas have been rejected, George Mason Law School Professor Nelson Lund argues that "there is now a large and well-settled body of case law strongly indicating that the...nominating commission should be struck down" under the Equal Protection Clause of the 14th Amendment to the U.S. Constitution.

A casual review of the relevant caselaw indicates that the plaintiffs have a very strong argument...based on U.S. Supreme Court precedent. Therein lies the problem. As Lund himself notes, these decisions were made over vigorous dissent (unrebutted by the court majority) that they were inconsistent with the original public understanding of the 14th Amendment (ratified in 1868).

As Justice John Marshall Harlan II wrote in his dissenting opinion in Reynolds v. Sims (1964):

> The failure of the Court to consider [the original public understanding] cannot be excused or explained by any concept of "developing"

> constitutionalism. It is meaningless to speak of constitutional "development" when both the language and history of the controlling provisions of the Constitution are wholly ignored...[T]he Court's action now bringing [suffrage] within the purview of the Fourteenth Amendment amounts to nothing less than an exercise of the amending power by this Court.
>
> So far as the Federal Constitution is concerned, the complaints in these cases should all have been dismissed below for failure to state a cause of action, because what has been alleged or proved shows no violation of any constitutional right.

The text of the 14th Amendment itself belies the notion that it mandates equal voting rights for everyone. For instance, Harlan noted that, irregardless of the 14th Amendment's guarantee of equal protection, Section 2 of that Amendment expressly allowed States the ability to deny the right of suffrage to black men, though it punished them for doing so by reducing their representation in the U.S. House. The right of suffrage was not extended to blacks until the 15th Amendment (1870), to women until the 19th Amendment (1920), or to eighteen-to-twenty-year-olds until the 26th Amendment (1971).

In addition to the text, Justice Harlan examined the original public understanding of the Amendment and concluded that: "The history of the adoption of the Fourteenth Amendment provides conclusive evidence that neither those who proposed nor those who ratified the Amendment believed that the Equal Protection Clause limited the power of the States to [regulate suffrage] as they saw fit. Moreover, the history demonstrates that the intention to leave this power undisturbed was deliberate, and was widely believed to be essential to the adoption of the Amendment."

For instance, John Bingham (R-OH), the author of the 14th Amendment's equal protection guarantee, acknowledged that: "To be sure, we all agree, and the great body of the people of this country agree, and the committee thus far in reporting measures of reconstruction agree, that the exercise of the elective franchise, though it be one of the privileges of a citizen of the Republic, is exclusively under the control of the States." (emphasis original)

Senator Jacob Howard (R-MI), who served on the committee which drafted the 14th Amendment, gave the following explanation of its meaning:

> The last two clauses of the first section of the amendment disable a State from depriving not merely a citizen of the United States, but any person, whoever he may be, of life, liberty, or property without due process of law, or from denying to him the equal protection of the laws of the State. This abolishes all class legislation in the States, and does away with the injustice of subjecting one caste of persons to a code not applicable to another. It prohibits the hanging of a black man for a crime for which the white man is not to be hanged. It protects the black man in his fundamental rights as

> a citizen with the same shield which it throws over the white man. Is it not time, Mr. President, that we extend to the black man, I had almost called it the poor privilege of the equal protection of the law? . . .
>
> But, sir, the first section of the proposed amendment does not give to either of these classes the right of voting. The right of suffrage is not, in law, one of the privileges or immunities thus secured by the Constitution. It is merely the creature of law. It has always been regarded in this country as the result of positive local law, not regarded as one of those fundamental rights lying at the basis of all society and without which a people cannot exist except as slaves, subject to a depostism [sic].

In short, as much as we may personally want the suit challenging Iowa's judicial selection process to prevail, such a result is not justified by the text or history of the 14th Amendment which explicitly excluded voting rights from its guarantee of equal protection. If the Amendment specifically left States with the ability to deprive blacks the right to vote, then certainly it leaves States free to limit the right to vote for commissioners.

In our eagerness to change the commission system, we must not become activists ourselves. The people of Iowa adopted this system, and it is long past due that the people of Iowa work to reform it. The inequality in the selection of commissioners is certainly something the General Assembly can remedy, but courts are powerless to do so under the 14th Amendment.

CONSTITUTIONAL PARENTAL RIGHTS?

(January 6, 2011)

On the final business day of 2010, the Iowa Supreme Court released its unanimous ruling in Ashenfelter v. Mulligan (2010) in which it held that the Constitution guaranteed parental rights, despite the fact that no such right exists in the text or original public understanding of either the U.S. or Iowa Constitutions.

Amy Mulligan, the daughter of Jerry and Susan Ashenfelter, separated from her husband in

December of 2007 and decided that it was not in her son's best interest to see his grandparents (her parents), the Ashenfelters. The Ashenfelters in turn filed a petition seeking grandparent visitation under the Iowa Code.

In prosecuting their suit, the Ashenfelters sought to obtain Amy's medical and mental health records in order to prove that she was an unfit parent incapable of adequately deciding who should have visitation with her child. Unsurprisingly, Amy asked the trial court to shield her records from discovery by the Ashenfelters.

The trial court ruled in favor of the Ashenfelters, but on appeal the Supreme Court reversed, holding that the records are privileged under Iowa Code section 622.10 and therefore undiscoverable in a lawsuit. Reasonable minds may disagree, as the trial court did, but at least the Court did not engage in the creation of new rights.

That is, until it proceeded to also conclude that such records were protected by Amy's constitutional right to privacy. There was no need for the Court to consider the constitutional issues as it had already ruled in Amy's favor based on Iowa statute, but apparently the temptation to rewrite the

Constitution at every opportunity is too great to resist.

Without discussing how it found this constitutional right to privacy, it merely cited a 1993 decision in which it had held that: "[T]he majority of [courts] hold that the right of privacy should extend to the patient records of mental health professionals...We join those courts that extend constitutional protection to such records."

While no one disputes the notion that one has a privacy interest in his or her medical records that should be protected by statute, it simply is not an enumerated right protected by either the federal or state constitutions. Rights created by judicial fiat with no basis in the original public understanding of the Constitution can be extended, restricted, and manipulated as the courts see fit.

Unfortunately, the Court didn't stop with reading into the Constitution a right of privacy that does not exist, but it also held that: "Amy's parental interests in the care, custody and control of [her son] is a fundamental liberty interest protected by the United States and Iowa Constitutions."

Again, no one disputes that parents have an indisputable right to raise their children as they see fit, but it does not exist in the text or original public understanding of either the U.S. or Iowa Constitutions. As Justice Scalia noted in his dissent in Troxel v. Granville (2000):

> In my view, a right of parents to direct the upbringing of their children is among the "unalienable Rights" with which the Declaration of Independence proclaims "all Men ... are endowed by their Creator." And in my view that right is also among the "othe[r] [rights] retained by the people" which the Ninth Amendment says the Constitution's enumeration of rights "shall not be construed to deny or disparage." The Declaration of Independence, however, is not a legal prescription conferring powers upon the courts; and the Constitution's refusal to "deny or disparage" other rights is far removed from affirming any one of them, and even farther removed from authorizing judges

to identify what they might be, and to enforce the judges' list against laws duly enacted by the people. Consequently, while I would think it entirely compatible with the commitment to representative democracy set forth in the founding documents to argue, in legislative chambers or in electoral campaigns, that the state has no power to interfere with parents' authority over the rearing of their children, I do not believe that the power which the Constitution confers upon me as a judge entitles me to deny legal effect to laws that (in my view) infringe upon what is (in my view) that unenumerated right...

Judicial vindication of "parental rights" under a Constitution that does not even mention them requires (as Justice Kennedy's opinion rightly points out) not only a judicially crafted definition of parents, but also-unless, as no one believes, the parental rights are to be absolute-judicially approved assessments of "harm to the child" and judicially defined gradations of other persons (grandparents, extended family, adoptive family in an adoption later found to be invalid, long-term guardians, etc.) who may have some claim against the wishes of the parents. If we embrace this unenumerated right, I think it obvious-whether we affirm or reverse the judgment here, or remand as Justice Stevens or Justice Kennedy would do-that we will be ushering in a new regime of judicially prescribed, and federally prescribed, family law. I have no reason to believe that federal judges will be better at this than state legislatures; and state legislatures have the great

> advantages of doing harm in a more circumscribed area, of being able to correct their mistakes in a flash, and of being removable by the people.

While the Iowa Supreme Court's decision legalizing same-sex marriage in Varnum v. Brien (2009) is certainly its most notorious example of judicial activism, the Court's continuing post-election performance has shown that it will continue to engage in this kind of behavior unless judicial reform is established that exposes and prevents activists from assuming the bench in the first place.

Until then, the Iowa Supreme Court appears unwilling to relinquish its self assigned role as social shepherds.

A CONSTITUTIONAL RIGHT TO CAPITALISM?

(April 16, 2012)

"[This case] reveals an ugly truth: America's cowboy capitalism was long ago disarmed by a democratic process increasingly dominated by powerful groups with economic interests antithetical to competitors and consumers. And the courts, from which the victims of burdensome regulation sought protection, have been negotiating the terms of surrender since the 1930s."

So argued Judge Janice Rogers Brown (joined by Chief Judge David Sentelle) in her recent concurring opinion in Hettinga v. United States (D.C. Cir. 2011). But despite her stirring political defense of capitalism, she failed to identify a single provision in the Constitution that guarantees the right to capitalism.

Though entirely sympathetic with the plaintiffs, she agreed with the majority because, "given the long-standing precedents in this area, no other result is possible" in this case but the denial of their claims. "No doubt they would have preferred a simpler [legal argument]—that the operation and production of their enterprises had been impermissibly collectivized—but a long line of constitutional adjudication precluded that claim."

While the result was foreordained by precedent, she concurred separately in order to urge the U.S. Supreme Court to overturn this "long line of constitutional adjudication." She decried, for instance, the Court's decision in Carolene Products (1938) to "relegate economic liberty to a lower echelon of constitutional protection than personal liberty, according restrictions on property rights only minimal review."

She concludes that, "the practical effect of rational basis review of economic regulation is the absence of any check on the group interests that all too often control the democratic process. It allows the legislature free rein to subjugate the common good and individual liberty to the electoral calculus of politicians, the whim of majorities, or the self-interest of factions."

Her solution lies not in "the hope of correction at the ballot box[, which] is purely illusory." Instead, she wants the courts "to consider the wisdom of legislative acts—at least to inquire whether its purpose and the means proposed are 'within legislative power.'" Such wise jurists would doubtless overturn statutes that "interfer[] with the rights of property and contract...; with the natural law of supply and demand."

The problem, however, is that the Constitution simply does not protect "the natural law of supply and demand" from the "addition to redistribution." Some theorists have argued that the Due Process Clauses's guarantee of liberty and property protects "the natural law of supply and demand."

As previously noted, the only right granted by the Clause was process—requiring the government to proceed according to constitutional and statutory provisions. It was never intended to strike down a law for violating "due process", but rather to make sure the due process required by existing laws was followed.

Other theorists have postulated that the Privileges and Immunities Clause protects the right to capitalism. However, that Clause merely guarantees that whatever rights and privileges are afforded by federal law cannot be denied by the States.

In short, the problem with Judge Brown's concurrence is that it requires judicial activism to enforce non-enumerated rights, setting up the courts as an unelected super-legislature second-guessing the democratic process. The better legal argument isn't that Congress used its power for socialist means, but that Congress doesn't have the power to begin with under a Constitution of limited, enumerated powers.

In cases, however, where Congress does in fact have the power to act, the only recourse lies at the ballot box. Though there is no constitutional presumption against Congressional regulation of economic activity, there should be an electoral presumption against such interference.

As Judge Brown noted in a 2000 speech before the Federalist Society chapter at the University of Chicago, "humanity's capacity for evil and tyranny is quite a real and quite as great as its capacity for reason and altruism...in politics, the...former tendency [may be] the stronger."

Because man, by his fallen nature, is evil, government is instituted to restrain evil by securing man's unalienable right to life, liberty, and property. However, because government is made up of fallen men, it restrains evil as much (if not more) by not acting as it does by acting.

Every act of legislation, therefore, should be greeted by voters with distrust and skepticism. As Ronald Reagan aptly remarked, the "nine most terrifying words in the English language are 'I'm from the government and I'm here to help.'" The mantra of every citizen should be Bob Novak's famous admonition—always love your country, but never trust your government.

A FAIR-WEATHERED KING
(October 26, 2012)

In what can only be described as an act of political cowardice, Iowa's most conservative member of Congress embraced an activist decision by the U.S. Supreme Court as "constitutional" and encouraged those who thought otherwise to do something "constructive."

At their fifth and final debate, Democrat Christie Vilsack challenged Congressman Steve King to make his position clear on "whether he believes that women in this community have the opportunity, have the right, the legal right to go into the drugstore down the street and fill a prescription for birth control pills or go out to New Opportunities and get some of the new long-acting reversible contraceptives at the local family planning clinic."

King replied that the attack "comes from me explaining something, and that is a case called Griswold v. Connecticut. That was 1965. That was when the Supreme Court said that there is a constitutional requirement that prohibited the States from banning the sale of contraceptives. I accept that decision as constitutional, okay. If anyone advised otherwise, I would tell them, 'Why don't you go on to something you can be constructive with?'"

But as Congressman King well knows, Griswold, by giving birth to the notion of an unenumerated constitutional right to privacy, became the jurisprudential sire of a "right" to an abortion (Roe v. Wade) and to homosexual behavior (Lawrence v. Texas). In fact, writing for the majority in Lawrence, Justice Kennedy noted that Griswold is "the most pertinent beginning point" in judicial lawmaking.

Lawrence, in turn, has been relied on by courts in decreeing a constitutional right to gay marriage. Both Goodridge v. Department of Public Health (Mass. 2003) and Perry v. Brown (N.D. Cal. 2010), for example, cited Lawrence nine times, while the Iowa Supreme Court cited it four times in Varnum v. Brien (2009).

How is it then that Congressman King, a vocal critic of judicial activism in general and of Varnum in particular, can call its act of jurisprudential inception constitutional? For if Griswold is constitutional, so to are its progeny of Roe, Lawrence, and Varnum. If courts are free to create new rights by judicial fiat in Griswold, then there is no room to criticize them when they continue to do so in later cases.

It becomes hypocritical to denounce courts who "claim omnipotent power to imagine and confer constitutional rights that 'were at one time unimagined'" in one case, but not do so in another. If it is "obvious [that the justices] feel empowered and will follow their whim in future decisions rather than the law" in Varnum, than it is equally as obvious in Griswold.

Until last week Thursday, Congressman King had recognized the unconstitutionality of Griswold, calling it a "manufactured, judicial activist right to privacy" in an appearance with David Barton on WallBuilders Live in March. At a House Judiciary Committee meeting in February, King had noted that the unenumerated right to privacy created by the Griswold Court became the "foundation for mandated abortion."

Instead of flip-flopping in support of judicial activism, Congressman King should have reiterated his speech on the floor of the House in March in which he stated that:

> No public official, no person who takes an oath to a constitution can be taking an oath to something that is amorphous, something that fluctuates and something that can change. The Constitution

has to be fixed in place. Guarantees aren't amorphous, Mr. Speaker. It is no guarantee if it's amorphous. It has to be fixed in place and fixed in time...It's impossible to take an oath to something that is amorphous, that's living and breathing...

[In Griswold], all non-enumerated powers are reserved for the States or the people, respectively. So the Constitution, I say, defines that the States had that power. But yet, the Supreme Court, in their imagination in 1965, created this right to privacy, a right to privacy fabricated out of whole cloth, didn't exist in the Constitution, doesn't exist today in the Constitution...

I say if you lived in Connecticut in 1965 and you wanted contraceptives, you could drive across the State line, or you

> could move to another State. That was the vision of the laboratories of the State experiment of the Founding Fathers. States' rights, Tenth Amendment...

As Justice Black noted in his Griswold dissent, "I like my privacy as well as the next one, but I am nevertheless compelled to admit that government has a right to invade it unless prohibited by some specific constitutional provision."

INDEX

ABOUT THE AUTHOR

Nathan W. Tucker is an author and attorney who lives in Iowa. He has been a regular columnist for The iowa Republican and the Tea Party Tribune, as well as a guest columnist for a number of media outlets. His previous books include the novel Letters from Cell No. 73 and the nonfiction book We the People: The Only Cure to Judicial Activism.

www.nathanwtucker.com

COMING NOVEMBER 2013:

JULIA'S CHRISTMAS CAROL

By Nathan W. Tucker

During the 2012 U.S. presidential election, the Obama campaign released the Life of Julia, a slideshow which chronicled the life of a woman as she lived off of the cradle-to-grave welfare state. This year she encounters the Ghosts of Christmases Past, Present, and Future on her journey towards redemption. Think Charles Dickens meets Henry Hazlitt.

Made in the USA
Monee, IL
06 November 2026

67981962R00177